Penguin Education

Penguin Modern Economics Tex
General Editor: B. J. McCormick

The Control of the Money Supply
A. D. Bain

A. D. Bain

The Control of the Money Supply

Third edition

Penguin Books

Penguin Books Ltd, Harmondsworth, Middlesex, England
Penguin Books, 625 Madison Avenue, New York, New York 10022, U.S.A.
Penguin Books Australia Ltd, Ringwood, Victoria, Australia
Penguin Books Canada Ltd, 2801 John Street, Markham, Ontario, Canada L3R 1B4
Penguin Books (N.Z.) Ltd, 182–190 Wairau Road, Auckland 10, New Zealand

First published 1970
Reprinted 1971
Second edition 1976
Reprinted 1978
Third edition 1980
Reprinted 1982

Copyright © A. D. Bain, 1970, 1976, 1980
All rights reserved

Made and printed in Great Britain by
Richard Clay (The Chaucer Press) Ltd,
Bungay, Suffolk
Set in Monotype Times

Except in the United States of America, this book is sold subject
to the condition that it shall not, by way of trade or otherwise, be lent,
re-sold, hired out, or otherwise circulated without the
publisher's prior consent in any form of binding or cover other than
that in which it is published and without a similar condition
including this condition being imposed on the subsequent purchaser

Penguin Modern Economics Texts

This volume is one in a series of unit texts designed to reduce the price of knowledge for students of economics in universities and colleges of higher education. The units may be used singly or in combination with other units to form attractive and unusual teaching programmes. The volumes will cover the major teaching areas but they will differ from conventional books in their attempt to chart and explore new directions in economic thinking. The traditional divisions of theory and applied, of positive and normative and of micro and macro will tend to be blurred as authors impose new and arresting ideas on the traditional corpus of economics. Some units will fall into conventional patterns of thought but many will transgress established beliefs.

Penguin Modern Economics Texts are published in units in order to achieve certain objectives. First, a large range of short texts at inexpensive prices gives the teacher flexibility in planning his course and recommending texts for it. Secondly, the pace at which important new work is published requires the project to be adaptable. Our plan allows a unit to be revised or a fresh unit to be added with maximum speed and minimal cost to the reader.

The international range of authorship will, it is hoped, bring out the richness and diversity in economic analysis and thinking.

B. J. MCC.

Contents

Editorial Foreword

One of the more compelling associations suggested by historical studies is that between a nation's supply of money and the money value of its national income. That such an association should exist is hardly surprising. Money is socially useful not for its own sake but simply for the work that it will do in facilitating exchange transactions in organized markets; it is evident that a given collection of exchange transactions can be conducted just as well with a smaller as with a larger number of pounds or dollars, provided that money prices are correspondingly diminished. The interesting question, therefore, is not to account for the existence of a statistical relationship between the supply of money and the level of national income, but to explain in what ways the economic forces that perpetuate this relationship work. Does the supply of money adjust automatically to increases in money national income brought about by independent increases in aggregate spending on goods or services? Or does the level of money national income respond automatically to increases in the supply of money brought about by the action of the monetary authorities? Or does the truth lie somewhere between these two extremes, sometimes in one direction, sometimes in the other, depending on circumstances?

Present knowledge seems to favour the last alternative, but the issues involved are complex and no definitive answers are possible at this time. This being so, it is obviously desirable that students of monetary economics understand and appreciate alternative points of view on the question 'Does money really matter?' To reach such an understanding, however, a student must first acquire detailed knowledge about the nature and working characteristics of actual financial and monetary institutions. Professor Bain's book admirably provides the required background information, and at the same time offers a careful and balanced assessment of currently controversial issues in the theory of monetary control.

R. W. C.

Preface to the Second Edition

Students of economics are often faced with conflicting theories and contradictory policy prescriptions, and nowhere is this more evident than in the field of money. Is monetary expansion the cause of inflation, or is it a consequence of other forces? And should inflation be attacked by monetary or other measures? The answers to these questions are of the utmost importance to policy-makers around the world. Yet professional economists are at loggerheads and cannot agree on the advice they give.

In preparing the second edition of this textbook I have tried to help students understand what the controversies are about. The book is not intended for the monetary specialist, who will need to go much more deeply into the literature. Its target is the second or third year economics student, who is familiar with the basic models of macroeconomics and wants to learn about money – its supply and demand, its influence on output and prices, and how it should be controlled. The illustrations are taken mainly from the British economy. But the book is not about Britain, and the theories discussed can be applied in a great variety of institutional settings.

Most of the book has been rewritten, and I have taken the opportunity to separate material that is specific to the UK from more general discussion. This has led to a clearer division between theory and application. The section on the supply of money has been revised; whereas previously a model of the supply of money in the UK prior to 1971 was presented, now the determinants of the money supply are analysed in a more general framework and the model is applied to the current situation in the UK. Other important changes are in the chapter on the relations between money, economic activity, and prices, which now contains sections dealing with non-bank financial institutions and with money and inflation. At the end of the book a new chapter on the role of monetary policy has been added.

On some sections which are new or substantially revised I have had the benefit of comments both from my students at the University of Stirling and from two of my colleagues, Dr P. M. Jackson and Mrs S. A. Shaw. These have undoubtedly helped to clarify the exposition, and I am indebted to all who have assisted me in this way. I should also like to express my thanks to my secretary, Mrs C. B. McIntosh, who has converted – with great speed and accuracy – my well-nigh indecipherable drafts into copy fit for the publisher and printer.

A. D. BAIN
21 November 1975

Note to the Third Edition

For this revision I have made a few changes to bring the statistical material relating to the UK up to date. The section in Chapter 3 on *Monetary control in practice* (pages 70–77) has been rewritten.

A. D. BAIN
June 1979

1 Introduction

Does money matter? In recent years the importance of the money supply has been a subject for continuing public debate in many countries. Persistent slow inflation and the attempts to attain high and stable levels of economic activity posed such intractable problems that politicians and economists were forced to review and reconsider the techniques adopted for controlling their economies. During the 1950s fiscal policy generally held the centre of the stage, although towards the end of that decade and in the 1960s there was a gradual revival in the use of monetary policy. The quickening pace of inflation on a world-wide scale in the early 1970s, the temporary boom in most commodity prices, and the massive increase in the price of oil, served to concentrate attention on a search for means of influencing prices. Existing methods of controlling economic activity through demand management seemed to have failed, and the efficacy of direct measures to control prices and incomes was hotly disputed. The influence of money on activity and prices has therefore been one of the central issues in recent economic controversy.

Practical interest in the relevance of the money supply coincided with a revival of interest amongst theoretical economists. Keynesian economics, while it attributed an important role to the money supply in determining the level of economic activity, undermined the notion that there was any simple link between the supply of money, the level of output and the price level. This Keynesian approach, which dominated economic thought throughout the 1950s and 1960s, was not accepted by all economists, particularly the group of monetary economists in Chicago working with Milton Friedman. Since the early 1950s these economists, and others influenced by them, have produced a steady stream of literature pointing to the conclusion that some more direct causal link may exist between money, prices and activity; and in the last decade this stream has grown into a flood. The arguments put forward and the interpretation of the evidence cited has not been left undisputed, and controversy about the weight to be attached to monetary policy is still raging.

A central proposition of the monetarist school is that the quantity of money has no influence on *real* variables. The volume of physical goods and services available to a community, the level of employment, and the goods and services earned in exchange for work (the *real* wage) are all determined by the community's natural resources, physical capital and labour supply: the only long-run impact of money is upon the general price level. Thus money can influence *nominal* values – the wage measured in units of money, such as pounds sterling, or the number of pounds that must be paid for particular goods and services – but cannot influence the actual quantities produced, earned or purchased.

While Keynesian economists might wish to qualify this proposition slightly they would not generally contest the assertion that *in the long run* substantial changes in the quantity of money will be reflected mainly in the price level rather than in output. But they would argue that *in the short run* changes in monetary conditions may have a considerable impact upon real variables, and that this is a matter of great importance for economic management. Furthermore, many would claim that changes in the money supply are themselves a reflection of other economic and social forces, and that policy prescriptions which emphasize the importance of monetary control may mislead by distracting attention from these more fundamental matters.

The main part of this book will cover five topics. First, we shall consider what determines the money supply, starting from the familiar credit multiplier model. We shall try to expose some of the inadequacies of this model and shall develop an approach which focuses on the demands of the general public and of the financial system for alternative financial assets, as well as upon the government and external factors as influences upon the supply of bank reserves. We then move on to the demand for money, dealing with different theoretical models and discussing the empirical evidence which has been obtained. The next topic concerns the link between money, economic activity and prices. Here we shall consider alternative views of how money influences economic activity and discuss some of the empirical results bearing upon this; we shall consider the importance of non-bank financial intermediaries in facilitating or hindering the transmission of monetary pressures to the economy generally, and we shall also discuss the connection between the growth of the money stock and inflation. From the mechanism through which monetary policy influences the economy it is natural to move on to the techniques employed in monetary control; and this discussion of the instruments of policy leads in turn to an examination of the monetary authorities'[1] objectives, of the targets which they seek to influence and of the indicators which they may employ as a measure of the need for action. We shall conclude by discussing contrasting views of the role of monetary policy in economic management.

We have attempted as far as possible to separate theoretical and empirical material in our discussion. The theoretical models are intended to be of wide and general applicability, though their detailed use will in most cases reflect, of course, the particular institutional environment. The empirical evidence has been drawn mainly from the UK and the USA, though for some topics, such as the effect of inflation on the demand for money, evidence has also been drawn from the experience of other countries. The empirical discussion should be taken as illustrative of the theoretical models discussed; for example, the chapter on bank deposits in Britain shows how the general model of money supply determination must be modified in order to apply it in one particular institutional environment. Students from other countries should consider what modifications to the theoretical models are required to make them applicable to their own particular situation.

Before going on to the main question under review it is necessary to discuss the meaning and definition of money, to examine the functions of financial institutions in general and some aspects

1. By the 'monetary authorities' we mean the institutions – usually the government and central bank in consultation – which determine what monetary policy will be.

of banks' behaviour in particular, and to provide some background of the history of monetary control in the UK. The remainder of this introductory chapter is devoted to this purpose.

Definition of 'money'

For theoretical purposes money is usually defined as any asset which performs simultaneously the functions of a medium of exchange, a unit of account and a store of value. In practice, however, there are many financial assets which perform these functions to a greater or lesser degree, and this makes for difficulties in obtaining an empirical measure of the stock of money. The borderline between monetary and non-monetary financial assets has never been clear; it has changed as the characteristics of financial assets altered and as more sophisticated payments practices developed. For example, disagreement about the nature of money – whether or not bank deposits as well as currency were properly treated as money – was at the root of much of the controversy preceding the Bank Charter Act of 1844 in the UK. In spite of a number of attempts in recent years to establish theoretical criteria for distinguishing between money and non-monetary financial assets, no clear-cut basis has yet emerged.

Currency in circulation performs all the functions of money and is invariably included in any definition of the money stock. Nowadays no one doubts that some bank deposits – *demand* deposits (or current accounts) which are repayable or transferable on demand – should also be treated as money; but there is still disagreement over the inclusion of *time* deposits (or deposit and savings accounts) with commercial banks, which are formally transferable only after a period of notice. Strictly speaking these deposits are not a medium of exchange, though in practice banks in many countries waive their legal right to notice and will permit these deposits to be used for payment. If time deposits are to be included in the definition of money there is a question whether the deposits of other financial institutions, such as building societies in the UK, should also be counted since they too are effectively repayable on demand. Alternatively these deposits, and time deposits with banks too if they are not in practice repayable on demand, may be classified into another group of assets called 'quasi-money', which share some but not all of the characteristics of money. There are other, more detailed issues which must be settled too before an empirical definition of the money stock can be formulated. For example, some of the deposit liabilities of the commercial banks may be in foreign currencies. Should they be counted as part of the money stock? And should a country's money stock be confined to deposits owned by residents, or should the deposits held by non-residents also be included?

In deciding on these questions we must remember that the concept of money has been constructed for use in economic analysis. We hope to identify relationships between money and other economic phenomena in which we are interested. It is by no means certain that the same definition will be the most suitable at all times and in all circumstances; institutions change their character as they seek out new types of business, and asset-holders change their behaviour in response to new opportunities. The boundary between money and non-money, wherever it is drawn, will be arbitrary and may seem unsatisfactory. For this reason, many countries compile several measures of 'money', comprising narrower or broader categories of assets. The narrowest category will usually include currency and bank deposits which can be regarded strictly as means of payment, while broader categories will also include other deposit liabilities of the banks and possibly some other financial institutions.

Money in the UK

In the UK two conventional methods of calculating the stock of money are now employed. The first, known as M_1, is a narrow measure of the money stock restricted to notes and coin in circulation outside the banks and the sterling sight deposits[1] of UK private-sector residents with the banking sector. This is an attempt to measure the total means of payment held by UK private residents. Two adjustments are made to the figures: deposits made by one bank with another are eliminated, and a

1. Sight deposits consist of current accounts and deposits which are at call or are placed overnight. Until May 1975 only current accounts were included in M_1.

deduction is made for transit items – sums which have already
been added to the payee's account but which have not yet been
subtracted from the payer's account, reflecting the time which
elapses between the payee paying a cheque he has received into
his bank account and that cheque passing through the bank
clearing system before the appropriate sum can be deducted from
the payer's account.[1] Where the demand for money deals mainly
with the demand for a means of payment M_1 is likely to be the
most suitable measure.

The second measure in the UK is known as Sterling M_3 and is
a much broader measure of the money stock, reflecting money's
store of value function as well as that of a medium of exchange.
It comprises M_1 with the addition of UK private residents'
sterling deposit accounts with banks, their deposits with the
discount houses, and the public sector's deposits with the banks.
M_3 is thus the total sterling deposits of domestic sectors with the
banking sector plus notes and coin in circulation with the public.
Where we are concerned with the behaviour of the banking
sector as suppliers of deposits, M_3 is much better suited to
analysis than M_1.[2]

The banking sector includes all the main banking organizations. These range from the London clearing, Scottish and
Northern Ireland banks – the main 'deposit banks' with extensive
branch networks, which dominate retail banking in Britain – to
the merchant banks, overseas banks and international consortia
which specialize in wholesale banking business, involving large
deposits and loans. The banking sector also includes the private

1. There are two further complications. Payments made by credit transfer
result in a deduction being made from the payer's account *before* the corresponding credit is added to the payee's account: these must be offset
against cheques in the course of collection. And by no means all payments
are to or from accounts with a credit, rather than a debit, balance. Since a
payment which merely changes a debit balance is not reflected in the total
of bank deposits only a proportion of the net transit items should be
deducted: in practice the proportion taken is 60 per cent.

2. In the United States it has also been common practice to calculate two
measures of the money stock – which correspond broadly with those published in the UK. They are M_1, comprising currency and demand deposits,
and M_2 which includes time deposits also. Adjustments have of course to be
made for transit items ('float') and certain other matters.

banking business of the Bank of England, the deposits of the discount market and deposits with the National Giro.

Deposits by the public sector – the central government, local authorities and public corporations – are not included in M_1. They are distinguished from private-sector deposits because the opportunities for centralized cash management within the public sector – particularly within the central government – curtail its demand for money; the behaviour of the public sector in regard to money holdings therefore differs from that of private organizations.

The private sector is divided into the banking sector and other private-sector residents – industrial and commercial companies, other (i.e. non-bank) financial institutions, and a residual category known in the UK as the personal sector, which includes not only households but also unincorporated businesses, farmers, and non-profit making bodies. Frequently we shall refer to the non-bank private sector as a whole simply as 'the public'.

The composition of the UK money stock at the end of 1978 is shown in Table 1.1. Currency in circulation at that time formed roughly one third of money as a means of payment, a proportion which has varied little in the last few years. In Britain, as in most developed countries, the monetary authorities do not attempt to

Table 1.1 UK Money Stock, December 1978

	£ million
1 Currency in circulation	8,904
2 Private-sector sterling sight deposits*	20,093
3 Less 60 per cent of transit items	1,462
4 M_1 (= 1 + 2 − 3)	27,535
5 Private-sector sterling time deposits	23,195
6 Public-sector sterling deposits	1,299
7 Sterling M_3 (= 4 + 5 + 6)	52,028

* Non-interest bearing: £16,122 million.
Source: *Financial Statistics*, April 1979, Table 7.1.

control the supply of currency, so the amount in circulation is demand-determined. Thus in studying money we shall be much more concerned with bank deposits. About a quarter of the banks' sight deposits are interest-bearing, and when these are added to the banks' sterling time deposits we can see that over 60 per cent of the banks' sterling deposit base is interest-bearing.

Banks and other financial institutions

Since bank deposits often form the greater part of the money stock it might seem natural to begin a study of money by considering the role which banks play in the economy. But in fact banks are simply one category drawn from the whole range of financial institutions, and by viewing them first in the context of financial institutions in general, rather than studying them in isolation, a much clearer picture of the factors which affect their business can be obtained.

Financial institutions are an integral part of the mechanism through which savings are made available to borrowers. Within any period of time the basic decision-making units within an economy – households, firms, public corporations, the government, foreigners and so on – can be classified into potential surplus and potential deficit units. Potential surplus units are those whose intended incomes or receipts exceed their intended expenditures, and deficit units intend to spend more than they receive. In the absence of financial institutions it would not always be easy for economic units to achieve their intended surplus or deficit positions. Potential borrowers wishing to spend more than their income would not find it easy to borrow, and potential savers wishing to spend less than they receive might not find any acceptable way to lend. Financial institutions, which issue their own liabilities to savers and use the funds they receive to lend to borrowers, exist to bridge this gap.

Financial intermediation is important because potential deficit units are frequently those which wish to engage in productive investment. Firms borrow to equip factories, households to build dwellings; and the fruit of these investments is a larger flow of income, which contributes to rising living standards. Prospective savers, whose incomes exceed what they want to spend on current consumption may not have the desire or the expertise to engage in productive investment themselves. If there were no financial institutions, they would either increase their consumption or hoard jewellery, gold or other precious metals. This practice, which is by no means unusual in countries with ill-developed financial institutions, inevitably curtails the amount of productive investment undertaken. By offering their own liabilities as an attractive alternative to immediate consumption or unproductive investment, financial institutions are able to channel the savings of surplus units to borrowers who can put them to good use.

Why, it may be asked, do savers themselves not lend directly to borrowers without the need for any intermediary? The answer lies in the different requirements of savers and borrowers, in ignorance, uncertainty and lack of experience. Borrowers often want to borrow substantial sums for long periods, while savers frequently want to lend small sums for short periods. Borrowers may want to take risks – a prospect which many savers find uncongenial. Savers may be unaware of potential borrowers or know very little about them, they may be uncertain and fearful of the risk of loss, and they may lack the ability and experience to assess the prospects of profit. Financial intermediaries increase the range of *financial instruments* available to savers and borrowers; they offer a variety of liabilities which are tailored to fit savers' preferences, and they lend the funds they receive on a variety of terms which satisfy the needs of particular types of borrowers. By pooling risks, by averaging the experience of many individuals, and by acquiring the expertise to assess the prospect of profit and risk of loss inherent in loans to potential borrowers, these institutions are often able to provide for the individual saver a combination of interest, ease of repayment, protection against loss and other terms on his savings that are better than he could obtain by lending to ultimate borrowers himself.

Since the majority of the assets in which financial intermediaries invest are also available to ultimate lenders, financial intermediaries can exist only by providing liabilities with special features – for example, liquidity in the case of the deposit-taking institutions and regular saving for old-age and insurance facilities in the case of the life insurance companies and pension funds. The provision of these special features imposes a constraint on each institution's choice of asset portfolio. Deposit-taking institutions must keep some liquid assets in case their depositors withdraw funds; life insurance companies hold some assets, e.g. loan stock and debentures, with a fixed monetary value. The existence of constraints on the choice of assets is thus a characteristic of financial institutions.

For our purposes it is convenient to divide financial institutions into three groups. The first is the central bank. This is generally the pivot of the entire financial system. Its most important liabilities are currency and deposits with it by the commercial banks. It acts as banker to these banks, and payments between them are made by drawing upon their accounts with the central bank.

The second group consists of the commercial banks and other deposit-taking institutions, such as savings banks and building societies. The essential feature of these institutions is that their liabilities can usually be converted into cash at short notice and have a fixed monetary value. Deposits with these institutions are therefore regarded as good substitutes for each other. As we have already seen, it is often difficult to draw a line between those which should be regarded as money and those which are not. The existence of financial institutions other than banks, whose deposits are good substitutes for bank deposits, has implications for both the theory and practice of monetary policy; this will be discussed in Chapter 6.

The third group consists of financial institutions which are directed to providing for long-term savings of the private sector. The post important media for this purpose are life assurance and pension schemes, particularly the latter. Saving for retirement is a very long-term objective, and savings held for this purpose are not generally highly substitutable with money.

Amongst the deposit-taking institutions our principal concern will be with banks. The distinctive features of bank deposits are their unquestioned and fixed monetary value and the ease with which they can be used to settle debts or be converted into cash. A bank's choice of assets is constrained by the need to ensure that its deposits retain these attributes. First and foremost a bank must not risk losing its depositors' funds, which means that its own capital and reserves must be sufficient to cover any foreseeable loss on the loans and other investments which it makes. Secondly, a bank must always hold or have access to sufficient cash to meet its customers' requirements for cash and to carry out their instructions to transfer funds to other banks without delay. This condition is satisfied partly by holding cash, partly by holding other highly liquid assets from which cash can be replenished, and possibly also by borrowing from other banks which have cash to spare. Banks must also hold cash to meet any unanticipated demand for loans by their customers. A persistent loss of cash involves more widespread adjustments in a bank's asset portfolio, such as reducing its holdings of investments, cutting back on new loans and reducing loan limits upon renegotiation.

A bank expects to earn a higher rate of return on loans and investments than on its more liquid assets; thus the balance of its portfolio affects the earnings which are available to meet the expenses incurred in running its business. To remain competitive a bank must earn enough on its assets to pay interest on deposits, to provide for any free (or undercharged) services to its customers, and to allow for profit on its own capital. A bank must therefore balance the need for liquidity against the desire for high earnings. In many countries convention or legislation ensures that banks maintain sufficient cash or liquid assets in their portfolios to protect their depositors from loss, though an upper limit on such holdings is not specified.

Banks' requirements for cash and liquid assets also play an important part in the mechanism of monetary control. Where legislation dictates the type and amount of cash or liquid assets which the banks must hold, and where the monetary authorities can control the supply of these assets, the authorities possess a powerful means of influencing the banking system. And even when neither legislation nor convention dictates any rigid relationships within banks' asset portfolios, they will adjust their portfolios in response to a change in the supply of liquid assets, although the reaction will probably be less prompt and less predictable than if the constraint were rigid. The significance of such liquid reserves will become apparent in Chapters 2 and 7 when the determinants of the volume of bank deposits and techniques of monetary control are discussed.

Financial institutions in the UK

We turn now to consider in more detail some of the institutions within each category in the UK. The central bank, the Bank of England, will not be discussed further here since its operations are considered in some detail in Chapter 3.

Amongst the deposit-taking institutions are the commercial banks, the discount houses, the National Savings Bank and the Trustee Savings Banks (TSB), building societies, hire-purchase finance houses and the National Giro.

The main liabilities of the commercial banks are deposits, whose most distinctive characteristic is the ease with which they can be used to make payments. As Table 1.1 shows under half of commercial bank deposits (including most public sector deposits) in the UK are *demand deposits* or *current accounts*. Current accounts do not generally bear interest, though banks often pay for them by providing free services for which they would otherwise charge. The balance, mainly *time deposits*, bear interest; in principle time deposits are repayable only after a period of notice has expired, though in practice this condition is often waived. Banks employ their funds in a variety of ways. They hold *cash* and balances with other banks to meet their depositors' needs for cash and to carry out depositors' instructions concerning payments; they lend *money at call* – loans repayable on demand or at short notice – to the discount market (see below) and to some borrowers; they hold *treasury bills* – bills which are sold at a discount, i.e a price less than their face value, by the government and which mature three months after the date of issue; they hold *commercial bills* which are issued by companies which want to borrow funds; they hold *gilt-edged stocks* (government securities); many banks lend funds to *local authorities* for periods which may vary from overnight to about two years; and they make *advances* or *loans* which may be secured by a charge on some of the borrower's assets or may be wholly unsecured. These bank assets are listed broadly in order of increasing return and decreasing liquidity.[1] The composition of bank asset portfolios is largely determined by a balance between the desire for a high rate of return on their funds and the need for liquidity so that they can meet any demands for the repayment of deposits or any increase in the loans which customers require.

The discount market is comprised of institutions – the discount houses – which specialize in borrowing large sums, usually at call and mainly from banks, and employing these funds in commercial bills, treasury bills, local authority bills and bonds, and gilt-edged stocks. As a result of the institutional arrangements which prevail in Britain the discount market plays an important part in government financing and in the mechanism through which short-term interest rates are controlled.

The liabilities of the National Savings Bank and the Trustee Savings Banks are also deposits repayable in limited amounts on demand and in larger amounts after a short period of notice. These savings banks invest their funds in central government and local authority debt. They specialize in providing savings facilities for people with relatively small incomes. Both offer two kinds of account. The ordinary account is used mainly for short-term saving, deposits have a high rate of turnover, and the rate of interest paid is low. The investment account is intended for longer-term savings and is open only to those who hold a minimum balance in the ordinary account. Turnover is low and the rate of interest paid is closely geared to the earnings on the banks' funds. Trustee savings banks also provide current account facilities, which are employed in the same way as current accounts with the commercial banks. Deposits in these accounts are not yet[2] regarded as part of the UK money stock.

Building societies specialize in making loans to house purchasers, usually taking a mortgage on the house as security. They too obtain their funds as interest-bearing deposits or shares, which in this case differ from deposits only in that there is a slightly greater risk of loss or delay in repayment. In practice building society

1. The sooner an asset can be turned into cash without significant capital loss the more liquid it is said to be.
2. The TSB will be assimilated into the banking sector in due course.

shares and deposits are also usually repayable on demand. As well as mortgages the building societies hold liquid assets, mainly loans to local authorities and marketable government securities. These act as a buffer which allows the societies to absorb the effects of a shortfall in receipts or abnormally high new mortgage lending; they also help to guarantee the liquidity of their shares and deposits.

The next group of deposit-taking institutions are the hire-purchase finance houses. Most of these take comparatively large deposits for periods varying from seven days to two years, and they also borrow from banks. Their funds are employed in a variety of forms of instalment credit – loans which are repayable by instalments over a fixed period – and in related activities. For the purpose of monetary control, most hire-purchase finance houses in the UK are now treated in the same way as banks.

The National Giro is a comparatively recent innovation. It is a state-run payments mechanism, comparable to and competitive with that provided by the banks. Deposits with the National Giro are held almost entirely for payments purposes and are not yet a significant part of the money supply.

Amongst this group of deposit-taking institutions the National Savings Bank, the Trustee Savings Banks and the building societies are concerned mainly with small savers; the discount market and finance houses deal in large deposits; and deposits with the commercial banks range from small to very large. Competition for both small and large deposits is keen. But although the rates offered for small deposits follow any major trend in interest rates, in some cases they are rather inflexible in the short-term and change only infrequently; whereas large deposits are placed in an active market at rates of interest which react rapidly to changes in supply or demand conditions. A feature of recent financial behaviour in the UK has however been a marked increase in the frequency with which interest payable on small deposits has been altered.

Long-term savings institutions in the UK consist of the life insurance companies, pension funds, investment and unit trusts. The life insurance companies and pension funds specialize in issuing liabilities which allow purchasers to shield themselves or their families from some of the financial consequences of early death or lengthy survival, and at the same time their liabilities provide a useful medium for regular long-term saving. The basic sum assured – at death or the end of some fixed period – by a life assurance policy is usually fixed, but there is often a variable addition to this basic amount which reflects the profitability of the insurance company's investments. Through proven expertise in investment, insurance companies are able to increase the demand for their liabilities. Pension schemes may also be for fixed sums of money, although it is now more common for such schemes to guarantee a pension related to the person's earnings in the years preceding retirement.

Life insurance companies and pension funds invest their funds mainly in assets which are expected to yield a high income over a long period; they have little need for liquidity since most of their liabilities are not repayable at short notice, although from time to time they may choose to invest in short-term assets to try to take advantage of some transient market situation. Their main assets are company *shares* and *debentures*, gilt-edged and local authority stocks, property, and loans secured by mortgages. Company shares and debentures require a little explanation. Theoretically a company's shareholders are its owners and their shares entitle them to a share in the dividends paid out of the profits the company makes. If a company is expected to be profitable, these shares, which carry the right to a stream of dividends, have a market value which reflects the current view about the stream of dividends the company is likely to pay in future.[1] Shares[2] consequently offer the prospect of a growing income over the years if the company is successful, but also carry the risk of loss if profitability falls. They also offer some protection against rising prices, since over the very long term it is not unreasonable to expect company profits, and hence dividends, to move approximately in line with the price level though government policies on pricing and dividends and changes in tax

1. The price of shares is also affected strongly by changes in the general level of interest rates and by speculative considerations.
2. Strictly, *ordinary* shares.

structure may disturb this relation for extended periods. (Investment in commercial property also offers protection against inflation because rents are likely to rise if other prices rise.) Company debentures, which bear a fixed rate of interest, are long-term liabilities issued by companies. They are usually secured on some of the company's physical assets. Although the life insurance companies and pension funds have reduced the proportion of their assets held in fixed interest securities in the last decade, these institutions are still very important holders of gilt-edged stocks and debentures.

The unit trusts and investment trusts issue liabilities with essentially the same characteristics as ordinary shares – though the investment trusts also have some long-term fixed interest liabilities – and invest their funds mainly in company shares. They offer their shareholders the advantages of reduced risk, because the trust's portfolio contains shares in many more companies than the individual could expect to hold himself, and of expert management, because by operating on a large scale the trust can devote substantial resources to assessing the prospects of particular companies and to judging the value of their shares.

In considering the assets of these financial institutions, most of the financial assets which ultimate lenders can hold have been mentioned. However, there has been one important omission – government non-marketable debt. Some of the deposits with the National Savings Bank and the Trustee Savings Banks – that part which is automatically lent to the government – are normally included in this category, but other major items which have not yet been considered are national savings certificates, British savings bonds, national development bonds, premium bonds and local authority loans and mortgages. The first three offer a variety of terms intended to appeal to savers; the rates of interest paid are changed only infrequently but an attempt is made to keep them broadly in line with market rates of interest (after allowing for any tax concessions). Government non-marketable debt is an important source of central government finance. Local authorities borrow very large sums in aggregate both from financial institutions and direct from the public. They pay the going market rates of interest, and since they accept sums com-

parable to those taken by banks or building societies from
private individuals, sometimes appear to be in active competition
with these institutions.

Monetary controls in the UK

A brief outline of the monetary controls which have been employed in Britain since the end of the war provides a useful background for the analysis in the chapters which follow (see Bank of
England, 1969). The formal control system remained virtually
unchanged for a twenty-five year period from 1946 until 1971,
but as we shall see, there was a gradual extension of requests and
directives to the banks, and in September 1971 a new system of
credit control was introduced. In the earlier period the main
deposit banks had to observe minimum cash and liquid assets
ratios, 8 per cent of total deposits for cash and 30 per cent (28 per
cent from the autumn of 1963) for liquid assets.[1] From 1961 the
authorities also made continuous use of Bank rate, which was
normally the minimum rate charged by the Bank of England for
advances to the discount market and which derived its importance
from its influence on interest rates generally: the clearing bank
deposit rate was tied to Bank rate, and many other interest rates
tended to move broadly in line with movements in Bank rate. As
managers of the National Debt the Bank of England also operated
continuously in the gilt-edged market, thereby influencing the
yields on government securities of all maturities. For almost the
entire period from 1951 on, the deposit banks were requested to
follow particular policies in their lending – to restrict the level of
bank advances or to discriminate in favour of some, or against
other, classes of borrower. For example in 1955 the Chancellor of
the Exchequer asked the London clearing and Scottish banks to
make a positive and significant reduction in their advances; there
were renewed requests concerning the level of advances in 1956
and 1957, and when in 1958 the banks were released from their
undertakings on advances the importance of providing credit for
export business was stressed. Again, in 1966 a Bank of England

1. The arrangements for the Scottish and Northern Ireland banks differed
in detail from the arrangements for the London clearing banks described
here.

press announcement stated that priority should be given to export finance, productive investment and temporary bridging finance for house purchase, in that order.

Throughout the 1950s requests related to advances and were addressed to the deposit banks. In 1960 and 1961 there were a number of innovations: a Special Deposit scheme (see Chapter 3), under which the banks had to make additional deposits with the Bank of England and which was intended to influence banks' behaviour by acting on their liquidity, was introduced; the growth of commercial bills as an instrument for company borrowing, which could be employed as a means of offsetting the effect of reductions in advances, was discouraged; and other banks were informed officially of the authorities' desire to encourage restraint in bank lending. Thus the scope of controls was widened with respect both to the type of asset and the range of financial institutions covered. From 1961 on there was a tendency to make controls more rigid and to apply them to a wider range of institutions whenever a tightening of credit seemed necessary. Requests were addressed to finance houses and insurance companies, ceilings were applied to each bank's advances, commercial bill holdings and acceptances, and restrictions were also placed on the amounts of commercial bills held by the discount houses. A Cash Deposits scheme, analogous to special deposits, was designed as a means of influencing the behaviour of the non-deposit banks, and was accepted by these banks although it was never in fact implemented.

In summary, from the early 1950s the Bank of England influenced the behaviour of all asset holders through their control of Bank rate and their operations in the gilt-edged market. The deposit banks observed cash and liquid assets ratios throughout, and as non-deposit banks and other financial institutions grew in importance direct controls were applied to them and also to the deposit banks. Finally, 'requests' concerning the level and direction of bank lending became a regular feature of monetary control in Britain.

As the range of controls extended it became steadily more apparent that they were discriminating against certain banks – the deposit banks – and that as a result partly of these controls and partly of self-imposed agreements on rates of interest paid and charged, these banks were at a competitive disadvantage. The lending limits applied to individual banks were also severely impeding competition between banks in Britain. As a result, the Bank of England produced a Discussion Paper entitled 'Competition and Credit Control' which proposed a revised system of credit control, and in the autumn of 1971 this system was introduced. Under it the deposit banks agreed to discontinue their practice of paying a common rate for small deposits, and all the banks become subject to a minimum ratio of $12\frac{1}{2}$ per cent between reserve assets and eligible liabilities (see Chapter 3). In addition the Bank retained the power to call special deposits from all banks. Special rules were applied to the discount houses and finance houses. Subsequently, the Bank of England abolished Bank rate and replaced it with a minimum lending rate. For a time this was a market-determined rate closely linked to other short-term interest rates, but more recently the Bank has reverted to the earlier practice of setting the rate autonomously. There have also been a number of other modifications. Although the initial objective was to do away with restrictions on individual banks in order to permit the credit market to operate freely, the Bank has found it necessary to continue to make requests concerning the direction of lending, for a time to set a maximum rate of interest payable for small deposits, and for extended periods to set a maximum rate of growth (without penalty) on the interest-bearing deposits of individual banks. The working of the present system will be discussed in detail in Chapter 3.

2 Money Supply Theory

In this chapter we begin with the traditional approach to the determination of the volume of bank deposits, in which deposits are linked to the reserves of the banking system. We shall then consider what factors influence the level of reserves and how the money supply as a whole is determined.

Fractional reserve systems

Bankers observe that they can lend out only the deposits they receive. So far as they are concerned the ability of their banks to attract deposits is the primary constraint on the level of their business. Economists, on the other hand, often assert that bank lending itself creates deposits. In their view bank deposits are a result of lending rather than a precondition for it; and the constraints which limit the growth of banks' assets and liabilities stem from the factors which operate to restrain their lending. The economists' assertion rests upon the following theoretical model.

Let us consider a highly simplified economy by making the following assumptions:

1 The only financial instruments are cash,[1] bank deposits and bank loans.
2 The banking sector consists of a single bank.
3 The non-bank public's financial assets consist of cash and deposits, and their demand for cash is fixed.
4 The bank's assets are cash and loans. The latter earns interest but the former does not. The bank aims to maximize its income subject to satisfying a liquidity constraint, which entails holding

1. Cash consists of currency and deposits with the central bank.

cash amounting to a minimum of 10 per cent of its deposit liabilities.[1]

5 The supply of cash is autonomous.

The effect of removing each of these assumptions will be discussed later.

Table 2.1 shows a series of hypothetical balance sheets for the banking sector. We assume initially that deposit liabilities of 100 are matched by 10 of cash and 90 of loans, giving a cash ratio of 10 per cent. This is shown in section A of Table 2.1. Suppose that the public acquire an extra 10 of cash, perhaps as a result of additional government expenditure. Since we have assumed that the public's demand for cash is fixed they deposit the 10 of cash with the banking sector, which then has 20 of cash and 110 deposits as shown in section B of Table 2.1. Now at 18·2 per cent the banking sector's ratio of cash to deposits is higher than the required minimum of 10 per cent and this is unprofitable because, while banks earn interest on loans, cash yields nothing and the sector's holding of cash needs only to be 11. The banks will therefore take steps to increase their loans by 9. If we suppose that the new borrowers withdraw cash up to the amount of their loans the banking sector's portfolio appears as in section C of Table 2.1 and with their cash ratio back to 10 per cent the banks are in an equilibrium situation.

But the public are not. Once again the public hold more cash than they want, because the borrowers will use their cash to make payments, and this means that the recipients will have excess cash holdings of 9. They get rid of their excess cash by depositing it with the banks and so increase bank deposits to 119 as shown in section D of Table 2.1. The banking sector's cash holding reverts to 20, and its cash ratio rises to 16·8 per cent – still higher than the equilibrium ratio of 10 per cent.

It is clear that this sequence in which the banking sector increases its loans and the public increase their deposits by returning the cash to the banks will continue until *both* the public *and* the banking sector are in equilibrium. So long as the public

1. That is, its reserves take the form of cash and it adheres to a 10 per cent reserve ratio.

Table 2.1 Hypothetical Balance Sheets for the Banking Sector

	Liabilities	Assets		Cash % ratio
A	Deposits 100	Cash	10	
		Loans	90	
	100		100	10
B	Deposits 110	Cash	20	
		Loans	90	
	110		110	18·2
C	Deposits 110	Cash	11	
		Loans	99	
	110		110	10
D	Deposits 119	Cash	20	
		Loans	99	
	119		119	16·8
E	Deposits 200	Cash	20	
		Loans	180	
	200		200	10

steadfastly refuse to hold any more cash this equilibrium will occur when the banking sector's required holdings of cash amount to 20, i.e. when deposits are 200 and loans are 180 (Table 2.1 section E).

The mechanism of deposit expansion has been illustrated in terms of a fixed *cash* reserve ratio, but is by no means confined to cash. A similar system can exist whenever banks maintain a fixed ratio of some asset or group of assets – 'reserves' – to their deposit liabilities: a change in their holdings of the specified assets will be associated with a proportionate change in their deposits. Moreover this kind of model can be extended to allow for different types of deposits, each with its own reserve ratio.

If a banking system works to a minimum ratio of reserves to deposit liabilities we say that it is a *fractional reserve system*. In such a system, if all the simplifying assumptions listed above applied and if r was the minimum ratio of reserves to deposits, the level of deposits D could not exceed $(1/r) \times C$, where C is the level of reserves; and if the system was operating at its minimum reserve ratio and a unit increment in its holding of reserves was received this would be associated with an increase in its deposits[1] amounting to $1/r$.

It should be noted that this theory begs a number of questions. Why does the bank stick to a constant reserve ratio? Why do the public not retain some of the extra cash? And, above all, why are the public willing to hold the additional bank deposits? It is assumed that if the public's holdings of bank deposits exceed what they would wish to hold permanently their attempts to regain equilibrium will involve purchases of goods, services or financial assets, with effects on output and prices which in due course will justify whatever level of bank deposits has been created. The assumptions about the nature of the financial market rule out any adjustment mechanism which might react back on the supply of bank reserves. This, as we shall see, is one of the model's limitations.

We turn now to consider the effect of relaxing the simplifying assumptions. Allowing for a greater variety of financial instruments does not alter the analysis provided that the supply of reserves remains exogenous and neither the public's demand for cash nor the bank's demand for reserves is affected. Nor is the assumption that the banking sector consists of a single bank in any way essential. In a system with many banks, provided that all the banks work to the same minimum reserve ratio, an increase in one bank's cash will encourage it to increase its loans and result in cash being paid into banks somewhere in the system; and these banks, finding themselves with excess cash, will take steps to increase their loans, so that the process will continue until the

1. If ΔD is the increase in deposits, in equilibrium $r\Delta D = 1$ or $\Delta D = 1/r$.

multiple expansion of deposits has taken place in the same way as before and no bank has excess reserves.

This is not to say that the value of r, the minimum reserve ratio, is unaffected by the structure of the banking system. If there are only a few banks and if they are large the stability of their total deposits is likely to be much greater than if they are many and small because the maximum net demand for cash resulting from short-term differences between payments into and out of their depositors' accounts rises less than in proportion to their total deposits and, because when the banks are few, a significant proportion of such payments represents transfers between accounts held with the same bank which do not involve any change in the bank's cash resources. Thus the value of r which the banks desired would be lower if the system was concentrated into a few banks than if the number was large. However, given the value of r which is appropriate to the structure of the banking system the proposition that deposits will rise by a maximum of $1/r$ times any increase in the system's reserve holdings remains true. Moreover, in banking systems to which this theory has been applied the reserve ratio is determined not so much by the individual requirements of banks for reserves as by conventional rules and legal obligations, and in such cases it is legitimate to treat r as a constant for all banks and to analyse the creation of money through the banking system as if it consisted of a single bank.

The assumption that the public's demand for cash is *fixed* in absolute terms is important because an increase in the public's cash holdings would reduce the reserves held by the banks. When this assumption is removed we must modify the analysis. Since both cash and bank deposits are used as a means of payment it seems plausible to assume that the public's demand for cash will rise with the demand for bank deposits, particularly if an expansion of the money supply and of bank loans is associated with an increase in the flow of income. The best way to integrate this into the theory is to assume that the public attempt to maintain a *constant ratio* of cash to deposits c. We shall continue to assume that the banks work to a fixed minimum cash ratio r. Let us investigate what happens if the public receive a unit increment in their cash holdings.

The public now find that their holdings of cash and deposits are out of balance: relative to deposits they have too much cash. To attain the desired ratio they must deposit part of the cash with their banks. In fact they will deposit $\frac{1}{1+c}$ with their banks and hold the remaining $\frac{c}{1+c}$ as cash. But this gives the banks excess cash, since they need to keep only the proportion r as reserves. They lend out the rest, $\frac{1-r}{1+c}$, to the public. Thus the first round unit increase in the public's cash holdings leads to a second round increase of $\frac{1-r}{1+c}$. This process continues until ultimately the public's cash holdings have risen by

$$\Delta C = \frac{c}{1+c}\left[1 + \frac{1-r}{1+c} + \left(\frac{1-r}{1+c}\right)^2 + \ldots\right]$$
$$= \frac{c}{c+r}.$$

The corresponding increase in bank deposits[1] is

$$\Delta D = \frac{1}{1+c}\left[1 + \frac{1-r}{1+c} + \left(\frac{1-r}{1+c}\right)^2 + \ldots\right]$$
$$= \frac{1}{c+r}.$$

The banks' loss of cash to the public in the course of a deposit expansion is known as the *internal cash drain*. It substantially reduces the multiple expansion of deposits. For example, if $r = 0.1$ and $c = 0.2$, the rise in deposits resulting from a unit increase in cash would be only 3.3, compared with 10 in the absence of any internal cash drain. Thus the extent to which banks can create deposits is limited not only by their own cash requirements but also by the cash requirements of the non-bank public.

The assumption that banks hold a fixed reserve ratio must now be reconsidered. Banks balance their need for liquidity against

1. Note that when there is no loss of cash to the public, $c = 0$ and $\Delta D = 1/r$ as before.

their desire for profits, and any increase in reserves entails forgoing profits, the opportunity cost being the excess of the yield on loans over any yield on reserves. If the return from loans falls during the process of deposit (and loan) expansion the banks' desired reserve ratio will tend to rise. Thus some flexibility in the reserve ratio is probable, and unless the public's demand for loans rises in conjunction with the banks' supply, thereby avoiding any reduction in the yield on loans, part of an increase in the supply of cash is likely to be absorbed by a higher reserve ratio. When this occurs the increase in reserves will not be reflected fully in bank deposit expansion.

Similar flexibility exists within the portfolio of the public. Thus the assumption of a constant ratio of cash to deposits made above is also too rigid, and changes in this ratio will influence the relationship between the supply of cash and the level of bank deposits.

The reserve base

Our final assumption, that the supply of cash can be treated as given, must now be considered. By and large the cash base of the financial system consists of liabilities of the central bank, in the form of either currency or deposits. To investigate the determinants of the cash base it is therefore necessary to examine the factors which influence central banks' assets and liabilities.

Table 2.2 Central Bank Assets and Liabilities

Liabilities	*Assets*
Currency	Private loans and securities
Commercial banks' reserves	Government loans and securities
Non-reserve liabilities	Gold and foreign exchange
Total liabilities	= Total assets

Table 2.2 lists these assets and liabilities, grouped into major categories. Private loans and securities represent loans made by the central bank to commercial banks or other private institutions and private securities purchased by the central bank. Central banks generally have considerable discretion over the volume of

these loans and securities. Loans to the government and government securities held may also be under the central bank's control, but it often happens that the exigencies of government financing effectively compel the central bank to increase this kind of asset. Gold and foreign exchange holdings reflect the central bank's functions in managing foreign exchange reserves; again, other policy commitments may lead the bank to have very little control over the level of this asset.

Changes in the asset total are necessarily matched by changes in the central bank's liabilities – generally in currency or in commercial bank reserves, which comprise the cash base of the banking system. For example, an increase in lending to the government to finance its spending allows the government to acquire currency from the central bank or draw on its account with the central bank, thus increasing the currency in circulation and the commercial banks' reserves. Non-reserve liabilities comprise the central bank's own net worth together with any other liabilities which are not treated as reserves by the banks. These may include compulsory deposits or holdings of other liabilities issued by the central bank, which may be held both by banks and by other institutions. The central bank usually has the power to vary these liabilities, and does so as one means of preventing asset changes from being fully reflected in the cash base or of otherwise bringing about a desired change in that base.

The need to provide finance for the government is a common cause of an increase in a central bank's assets. How much finance is required depends on the government's expenditure, the funds raised through taxation, and on borrowing from sources other than the banking system; the residue is provided by the banks, including the central bank. Political conditions frequently lead governments to spend much more than they can finance through taxation or by market borrowing, and in the last resort central banks are the servants of their governments and are compelled, however unwillingly, to provide the finance they need.

The amount the government can borrow from outside the banking system depends upon the terms on which the government attempts to obtain finance. The higher the interest rates offered by the government the more they can expect to raise from the public, and banks too will vary their holdings of government securities according to the return they expect to obtain. Thus the residue left for the central bank is not determined solely by the size of the government's borrowing requirements, but is influenced also by the preferences of both the commercial banks and the public.

Central banks also usually manage their countries' gold and foreign exchange reserves, and sustained surpluses or deficits in the balance of payments are reflected in the central bank's holdings of foreign exchange. If a country is running a surplus on its balance of payments, the commercial banks acquire foreign exchange and sell it to the central bank; commercial banks' reserves and the central bank's holdings of foreign exchange thus rise by equal amounts. Moreover, if domestic interest rates differ from the ruling level in other countries, short-term capital movements in response to interest differentials may be significant.

The importance of foreign exchange flows for the central bank's assets and for the commercial banks' reserves depends on the country's exchange rate policy. At one extreme, if the country allows its exchange rate to be determined entirely by the market, without any intervention at all by the monetary authorities, there will be no changes in the central bank's foreign assets. At the other extreme, if the country ties its currency rigidly to that of some other country, with a permanently fixed rate of exchange, the central bank will be a passive recipient or supplier of foreign exchange, in amounts which are outside its control; and any attempt to create financial conditions which differ from those in the partner country will be doomed to failure, since international short-term capital flows will substitute for any shortage or surplus of domestic funds. In between, floating exchange rates, with some intervention by central banks to prevent sharp changes in the rate, still allow the central bank to avoid large foreign exchange flows, whereas fixed but adjustable rates approximate more closely to permanently fixed rates,[1] with the added problem

1. Fixed rate systems generally allow the exchange rate to move within a narrow band, thus allowing some uncertainty as to the precise future rate of exchange, which helps to discourage short-term capital flows.

of potentially massive foreign exchange flows if a change in the exchange parity is anticipated.[1]

We have already seen how the public's holdings of currency affect the commercial banks' reserves. The central bank is usually responsible for maintaining a country's supply of currency, and in normal circumstances it is put into the hands of the public through the medium of the banks. The banks purchase currency from the central bank by drawing on their deposits with it, and the public acquire currency by drawing on their deposits with the banks. The size of the central bank's currency liability is therefore determined by the private sector's demand for currency.

Demand for currency, both by the banks to meet their customers' future requirements and by the public, is by no means steady. It varies according to the day of the week and the season of the year, with for example seasonal peaks during holiday periods. If the central bank took no action these fluctuations would be reflected in the commercial banks' reserves, irrespective of the authorities' desire to encourage or discourage monetary expansion. To avoid this the monetary authorities usually take action automatically to offset the effect of changes in currency holdings by buying or selling securities.

In our model of a fractional reserve system the public's holdings of currency were assumed to be a constant proportion of bank deposits. In reality the relationship is more complex. The rate of interest on currency is zero, but bank deposits often bear interest, and the public's preferences for both currency and bank deposits depend on the interest yield and on other interest rates. These interest rates are variable in the short-run, and cause movements in the cash to deposits ratio.[2]

1. Central banks generally intervene in exchange markets in an effort to offset erratic short-run surpluses or shortages of foreign exchange. Even though payments and receipts may be in approximate balance on a yearly basis, seasonal surpluses or deficits are common and there may be sharp erratic movements on a day-to-day basis. When this happens, central banks often offset the effect of foreign exchange transactions on the commercial banks' reserves by buying or selling equivalent amounts of other securities.

2. Note that the public's demand for government securities and consequently the size of the cash base are also affected. Thus the cash base and the cash to deposits ratio are not independent.

The government's financing needs, gains or losses of foreign exchange, and changes in the public's demand for currency, all react on the commercial banks' reserves with the central bank. When the net effect is large there may be precious little that the central bank can do about it. Nevertheless, the central bank does have a degree of discretion over some categories of assets and may also be able to alter the level of other non-reserve liabilities. We shall leave a detailed examination of the methods employed until Chapter 7 and shall simply note their main characteristics.

The central bank is free to make loans to the private sector and, where adequate markets exist, to buy or sell government securities – a technique know as *open-market operations*. By expanding loans or purchasing securities the central bank can always increase its own assets and the commercial banks' reserves. A reverse movement is not always so easy. A loan portfolio cannot be cut significantly unless it is both large and liquid, and sales of securities depend on finding willing buyers at prices which the bank is prepared to accept. When the government itself is borrowing heavily in the market the central bank may be quite unable to sell government securities from its own portfolio on tolerable terms. Open-market operations are the usual means of smoothing out the effects on the banks' reserves of short-term fluctuations in foreign exchange holdings and in the public's demand for currency.

Failing this, the central bank may resort to compulsion. To avoid an increase in the commercial banks' reserves the central bank may compel them (and other institutions) to acquire some of its liabilities, of a kind which cannot be treated as reserves. This usually occurs when government borrowing is leading to a rapid expansion of the central bank's assets and amounts, in effect, to compulsory subscriptions to government loans by the institutions concerned.[1] If subsequently the central bank wishes to expand the commercial banks' reserves the obligation to hold these non-reserve liabilities can be reduced or eliminated.

1. Loans via the central bank may be preferred to direct loans to the government, since it allows the government's demands to be disguised as a monetary control measure.

The level of bank deposits

We have now seen that while the commercial banks' reserves are strongly influenced by the authorities' policy commitments and objectives – the exchange rate régime, the government's borrowing requirement, and the interest rates offered on government securities – the reserve level is not wholly determined by them. The asset preferences of the general public and the banks, as reflected in their demand for government securities and currency, are also important. Since these preferences extend to the entire balance sheets of the public and the banks, and since the levels of bank deposits and of all other assets and liabilities must be in equilibrium, it makes little sense to argue that the level of reserves *determines* the level of bank deposits. Rather, the equilibrium levels of both are determined simultaneously within the system, and the process of adjustment to some disturbances will generally involve changes in both reserves and deposits until the equilibrium relationship obtains.

This view of the determination of the level of bank deposits reflects the truism that in a free market the authorities can fix either the prices (interest rates) or the quantities of the securities in which they deal, but not both. If they determine the interest rates offered on government securities, they cannot determine the size of the public's holdings.

The authorities could adopt an alternative strategy, fixing the level of the banks' reserves and buying or selling securities at whatever prices were necessary to achieve this end; and the notion that the volume of bank deposits is determined through a fractional reserve mechanism rests on the assumption that they do follow such a strategy, But there are two reasons why we might doubt that this is realistic. First, in many countries the possibility of international short-term capital flows compels the authorities to have regard to interest rate levels in the rest of the world. Such considerations can be ignored only if the authorities are indifferent to the level of the exchange rate or if capital controls prevent international capital movements. Secondly, if the authorities did select a target for the level of bank reserves it is difficult to believe that it would not be calculated by reference to some target level of bank deposits, in which case it would be more accurate to say that deposits determined reserves rather than the other way round.

Let us consider therefore how the system might react to a once and for all increase of 10 units in government spending financed initially by borrowing from the central bank. The cash base would therefore be increased by 10 units. Suppose that when the public receive payments from the government these comprise 1 unit of currency and 9 units of bank deposits, and suppose that the banks have a reserve ratio of 25 per cent. The initial impacts on the balance sheets of the public, commercial banks, central bank and government are shown in Table 2.3.

Table 2.3 Hypothetical Response to Government Borrowing – Initial Situation

Public				Commercial Banks			
Liabilities		*Assets*		*Liabilities*		*Assets*	
Borrowing from banks	Nil	Currency	+1	Deposits	+9	Cash	+9
Net worth	+10	Bank deposits	+9			Government securities	Nil
		Government securities	Nil			Loans	Nil
	+10		+10		+9		+9

Central Bank				Government		
Liabilities		*Assets*		*Liabilities*		
Currency	+1	Loans to government	+10	Borrowing from central bank	+10	
Banks' reserves	+9			Government securities	Nil	
	+10		+10		+10	

This situation will not last. First, if the public generally hold part of their asset portfolios in the form of government securities, they will gradually reduce their deposits and buy securities, thus allowing the government to curtail its dependence on central bank finance.[1] Secondly, the banks too may typically hold

1. We assume that the authorities fix the rate of interest on government securities at some target level.

government securities in their asset portfolios, in which case the government's dependence on central bank finance will be further reduced as the banks adjust their portfolios. If the public and banks hold, say, 10 per cent and $12\frac{1}{2}$ per cent of their assets as government securities respectively, before taking account of any credit multiplier effects, we have the position shown in Table 2.4.

Table 2.4 Hypothetical Response to Government Borrowing – Intermediate Situation

Public				Commercial Banks			
Liabilities		Assets		Liabilities		Assets	
Borrowing from banks	Nil	Currency	+1	Deposits	+8	Cash	+7
Net worth	+10	Bank deposits	+8			Government securities	+1
		Government securities	+1			Loans	Nil
	+10		+10		+8		+8

Central Bank				Government			
Liabilities		Assets		Liabilities			
Currency	+1	Loans to government	+8	Borrowing from central bank	+8		
Banks' reserves	+7			Government securities	+2		
	+8		+8		+10		

This is not the end of the story, because the banks' required reserves are only 2 and they have excess reserves of 5. They are therefore able to increase their other lending by this amount, and if they do so the process is repeated until the public and the banks have both reached a situation in which their portfolios are in equilibrium. This gives the final situation shown in Table 2.5.

This example shows how the choice of assets by the public and the banks influences both the process of adjustment and the ultimate equilibrium position. It goes beyond the standard model of a fractional reserve system, because while that model allows for the holding of cash by both the public and the banks it does not allow for the effect of the public's and banks' asset choice on the size of the cash base. Thus in this example, during

Table 2.5 Hypothetical Response to Government Borrowing –
Final Situation

Public			Commercial Banks		
Liabilities	Assets		Liabilities	Assets	
Borrowing from banks +10	Currency	+2	Deposits +16	Cash	+4
Net worth +10	Bank deposits	+16		Government securities	+2
	Government securities	+2		Loans	+10
+20		+20	+16		+16

Central Bank			Government	
Liabilities	Assets		Liabilities	
Currency +2	Loans to government	+6	Borrowing from central bank	+6
Banks' reserves +4			Government securities	+4
+6		+6		+10

the process of adjustment the cash base *contracted*: initially it
increased by 10 units as a result of the government expenditure,
but ultimately this had fallen back to 6 units. The straightforward
model of a fractional reserve system, in which the cash base is
treated as autonomous, is therefore inappropriate if the preferences of the public or the banks affect its size.[1]

This account of the process of adjustment is oversimplified. In
disposing of their funds neither banks nor the general public
automatically allocate fixed proportions to different categories of
asset. On the contrary, as noted above the disposition of funds
depends on the relative rates of return anticipated from each
category of asset. Thus, as loans expand banks may anticipate a
lower rate of return, and choose instead to increase their holdings
of cash and government securities and to cut the interest they pay

1. It is, of course, still true that the ultimate increase in deposits is $\frac{1}{c + r}$
times the final increase in the cash base: in the example $c = 0.125$ and
$r = 0.25$, and, with a final increase of 6 in cash, deposits must rise by
$\frac{1}{0.375} \times 6 = 16$. The point is that the increase in cash cannot be treated
as autonomous.

on (interest-bearing) deposits. The public would then find that securities were relatively attractive and increase their holdings. The assumption that the banks and the public will hold the different categories of asset in fixed ratios in their portfolio can be justified in an equilibrium situation, but is likely to be unwarranted in the short run.

This may be particulary noticeable if the central bank embarks upon a contractionary policy by selling securities and thus reducing the commercial banks' reserves. The banks which lose reserves initially (because their customers buy the securities sold by the authorities) will seek to rebuild them by selling securities from their own portfolios or cutting back loans and purchasing additional reserve assets with the proceeds. The shortage of reserves spreads through the system, and the process ensures that the yield from the securities and loans rises. The opportunity cost of holding reserves is therefore increased, and provided that they are not already holding the absolute minimum of reserves the banks will allow their free reserves (i.e. those in excess of the minimum) to absorb part of the reduction. But there will still be some tendency for the banks to contract their higher-yielding assets.

Within their earning assets the banks are likely to give priority to meeting demands from their customers for loan finance, since their profitability in the long run depends upon maintaining good customer relations, and a satisfied customer this year means more profits next year. Consequently, the reduction in banks' earning assets is likely to be concentrated mainly upon their holdings of securities. Whether this raises interest rates further depends upon the actions of the authorities. If they stay out of the market, securities sold by the banks must be purchased by the general public, and interest rates will rise; but if the authorities decide to prevent a further rise in interest rates, they must themselves purchase securities in the market thereby partially offsetting the initial reduction in the reserve base.

The general public too must be content with their portfolios of assets and liabilities. The amount of bank deposits they want to hold depends *inter alia* on the level of their wealth, the yields available to them from holding other assets, and the cost and availability of borrowed funds. The initial open market operation will itself cause a rise in security yields, since the public have to be induced to exchange securities for bank deposits. Any sales of securities by the banks will add to the pressure on interest rates, and, if the contraction of the reserve base causes the banks to restrict their lending to the private sector, the general public's demand for financial assets (including government securities) will also be reduced because some will choose to finance expenditure by running down these assets instead of borrowing. As we have already seen, other things being equal, a fall in the public's demand for government securities increases the reserve base.

The behaviour of the foreign sector is also important. If the response to a rise in domestic interest rates is an inflow of funds from abroad the authorities are bound to increase the supply of reserves to match the rise in their foreign exchange holdings. Nevertheless, in these circumstances, even though the banks have access to reserves, they will still be under some pressure to sell securities and contract credit because the cost of their funds will have increased.

Provided that the authorities do not engage in further open-market sales of securities, the end result depends upon how the public choose to adjust their portfolios in response to changed financial conditions, on how far the banks can rebuild their reserves by borrowing from abroad, and on how far they accommodate themselves by lowering their reserve ratios. If the authorities take a view about the desired level of interest rates they are bound to acquiesce in these reactions: the level of bank deposits and the reserve base are then determined simultaneously by the authorities' interest-rate targets, overseas interest rates, and the public and banks' portfolio preferences. It is only if the authorities subordinate other policy objectives to influencing the money supply, and so take action to compensate for reserve inflows and a reduction in the desired reserve ratio, that the authorities determine the level of bank deposits.

The determinants of the money supply

So far we have concentrated on the reserve base and on the level of bank deposits – the major component of the money supply.

To explain the size of the money stock we must add the supply of currency in circulation. This is demand-determined, and is usually closely related to the level of income in the economy. Since many central banks treat currency and the banks' reserve assets separately and, as we have seen, do not allow fluctuations in the demand for currency to influence the banks' holdings of reserves, the supply of currency can be treated as independent of the level of bank deposits in the short run.

In the long run, however, the cash to deposits ratio is determined largely by the public's preferences for these two kinds of financial asset, and provided that the cash base as a whole can be treated as autonomous – a major proviso – the standard model of a fractional reserve system can be employed to explain the money supply. Of course, where different reserve ratios apply to different types of deposit, some modifications to the basic model are needed. Nevertheless, it provides the foundation of models which have been applied to the banking systems of many countries at various times, and a monumental historical study of the money supply in the United States by Friedman and Schwartz (1963a) makes use of a series of versions of this theory, each of which is intended to reflect conditions prevailing at the time.

Friedman and Schwartz focus on three factors, the supply of 'high-powered' money H which comprises both the reserves of the banks and currency in circulation (cash, as we have called it), the banks' reserve ratio r, and the public's currency to deposits ratio c. Let M be the money supply, C be currency in circulation, D be bank deposits, and R be bank reserves. Then, by definition of the money supply and high-powered money respectively

$$M = C + D \tag{1}$$
$$H = C + R. \tag{2}$$

Dividing (1) by (2) gives

$$\frac{M}{H} = \frac{C + D}{C + R}$$
$$= \frac{C/D + 1}{C/D + R/D}$$
$$= \frac{c + 1}{c + r}. \tag{3}$$

Hence

$$M = H\left[\frac{1+c}{c+r}\right]. \tag{4}$$

H, c, and r are known as the *proximate determinants* of the money supply.[1]

The theory is useful when the factors which determine H, c and r can be identified and are independent. Friedman and Schwartz are able to analyse separately the factors which have affected each of the proximate determinants, and in some periods a change in any one of them could take place without affecting the others. The model has proved to be of both analytical and predictive value in the institutional environments which existed in some periods in the United States.

Nevertheless, the proviso that H must be autonomous and determined independently of c and r is crucial. If, as a result of central bank practice, H adjusts to compensate for changes in c or r, or if H is allowed to react passively to changes in M, theories which treat the asset preferences of the banks and the public explicitly are more fruitful.

1. Note that for a unit change in H

$$\Delta M = \frac{1+c}{c+r}$$
$$= \frac{c}{c+r} + \frac{1}{c+r}$$
$$= \Delta C + \Delta D$$

as derived on page 37 above.

3 Bank Deposits in Britain

In the previous chapter we examined in general terms the factors which bear upon the determination of the money supply in a country, without confining the analysis to the specific institutional framework of the United Kingdom. The object of this chapter is to show how the theoretical model which we have discussed can be applied to the circumstances found in Britain today. We shall begin therefore by outlining the main features of the scheme which has prevailed since September 1971 – the reserve base, eligible liabilities and special deposits – and shall consider some of the complications caused by the position and functions of the discount market. We shall then discuss the ways in which Bank of England operations are carried out and go on to examine the constraints upon monetary policy which arise from inflows or outflows of foreign funds. Finally, we shall see how the system has worked in practice and consider how experience has led to some modifications and extensions.

The scheme in outline

In the United Kingdom banks and finance houses are required to hold 'reserve assets' amounting to a minimum of $12\frac{1}{2}$ per cent (10 per cent for finance houses) of 'eligible liabilities,' and in addition they may be required to make 'special deposits' with the Bank of England. By varying the quantity of reserve assets available to the banking system the Bank of England can influence the interest rates on short-term assets and so induce changes in the banks' lending policies. The public's willingness to hold the banks' 'eligible liabilities' – broadly, their deposits – is also affected, and this in turn is reflected in the size and composition of the banks' asset portfolios. The main techniques for influencing reserve assets are open-market operations and special deposits.

Before this scheme was introduced a situation had gradually developed under which individual banks were obliged to restrict their lending within defined limits and were asked to give priority to some borrowers whilst denying credit to others. The main deposit banks were also obliged to hold specified proportions of certain assets in their portfolios: in particular, they were required to hold minimum proportions of cash and liquid assets. This put them at a competitive disadvantage in comparison with less rigidly controlled banks. The new system was designed to put all banks on an equal footing and to allow bankers to compete freely with one another following their own commercial judgement. All banks were to be subject to the same regulations and the authorities were to control the system by intervening in markets rather than issuing instructions to institutions. It was, however, recognized from the beginning that more detailed intervention might seem desirable, and as we shall see later this has in fact occurred.

Reserve assets

In the United Kingdom reserve assets are not confined to the liabilities of the Bank of England. The reserve asset ratio now employed evolved from the liquid assets ratio which was formerly applied to the London clearing and Scottish banks, and both the choice of assets designated as 'reserve assets' and the definition of 'eligible liabilities' reflect the historical origins of the scheme. Reserve assets comprise the following items:

1 balances with the Bank of England (other than special deposits);
2 treasury bills
3 money at call with the London Money Market;
4 gilt-edged stocks, with one year or less to maturity;
5 local authority bills eligible for rediscount at the Bank of England;
6 commercial bills eligible for rediscount at the Bank of England, up to a maximum of 2 per cent of total eligible liabilities.

With the exception of gilt-edged stocks maturing within one year, all these assets were previously treated as liquid assets by the banks. A significant omission from the reserve asset category is currency held by the banks in their branches or in transit to and from them. Although currency is undoubtedly liquid, and used to be treated as part of 'liquid' assets, it is now regarded as part of a bank's stock-in-trade. The deposit banks, with branches spread widely over the country, need to hold substantial amounts of currency to support their deposit business, but other banks such as the merchant banks whose deposits are generally taken in large sums require proportionately much smaller holdings of currency.

Before considering the implications of this choice of assets some comment on a number of the individual categories is required. Balances at the Bank of England exclude special deposits, which are of course treated separately, and are held mainly by the deposit banks for the purpose of clearing the daily net credit or debit transactions which arise between them. The clearing banks are subject to the additional restriction that each bank's *average* balance with the Bank of England should be not less that $1\frac{1}{2}$ per cent of its deposits – this provision is intended to assist the authorities in their day-to-day operations in the money market by allowing them to estimate closely the amount of cash required.

Money at call with the London Money Market was traditionally the first line reserve held by the banks on which they could call if they were short of cash. Although, as we shall see, treating money at call as a reserve asset causes the authorities some problems, this category bulks very large in the total of reserve assets and it would have been unreasonable to exclude it. Call money is not confined to balances with members of the London Discount Market Association, but also includes balances held with firms carrying on similar business and certain firms concerned with the gilt-edged market. To qualify as a reserve asset all call money must be secured.

Reserve assets include gilt-edged stocks with one year or less to maturity. That these stocks are highly liquid is indisputable, because as part of their normal debt financing operations the authorities are always prepared to buy in stocks some time before maturity in order to avoid very large cash payments on the date when the stock is due to be repaid. It therefore makes sense to treat gilt-edged stocks approaching maturity on the same basis as the treasury bills which would replace them if they were bought in, and the (arbitrary) dividing line at one year probably reflects the authorities' present practice.

The local authority and commercial bills included within reserve assets also represent an immediate source of cash to the banking system, since they count as reserve assets only if they are eligible for rediscount at the Bank of England. It is worth noticing that the Bank of England has indirect control over the volume of local authority bills in issue, and that the volume of commercial bills which may be treated as reserve assets is limited to a maximum of 2 per cent of the total eligible liabilities of any bank.

In an ideal system changes in the quantity of reserve assets would be very much at the behest of the authorities. In this respect the British system is by no means ideal. The reserve asset category includes liabilities of the private as well as of the public sector, the position of the discount market extends indirectly the range of assets which contribute to reserve assets, and a substantial volume of reserve assets, which could in certain circumstances be attracted by the banks, is normally held outside the banking system. From the standpoint of monetary control all of these limitations may at times be important. An expansion of commercial bill holdings would be a threat to the Bank of England's control of the reserve base if the banks initially held substantially less than the 2 per cent limit. Money at call with the discount market gives rise to problems, because the discount houses can hold with it assets such as sterling certificates of deposit or additional commercial bills which would not count as reserve assets in the banks' own portfolios, thereby effectively extending the range of reserve assets. Special arrangements, which are discussed below, have therefore had to be made for the discount market. Assets of a kind included in reserve assets, which are held outside the banking sector, could also pose problems for the authorities since, if the banks are short of reserve assets the yields on these securities (gilt-edged stocks with less than one year to maturity) will fall and holders will have an incentive to switch out of these stocks into higher yielding liquid assets, such as certificates of deposit with the banks.

Table 3.1 shows the composition of reserve assets in December 1978. At that time over 50 per cent consisted of money at call,

Table 3.1 Composition of Reserve Assets: December 1978

	£m	%
Balances with Bank of England	410	6·8
UK and Northern Ireland treasury bills	838	13·7
Money at call	3,222	52·5
British government securities up to one year to final maturity	700	11·4
Local authority bills	148	2·4
Commercial bills	804	13·1
Total	6,132	100·0

Source: *Financial Statistics*, April 1979, Table 6.6.

about 15 per cent was in commercial and local authority bills, and the balance was divided between treasury bills, British government securities and balances with the Bank of England.

Eligible liabilities

In broad terms the eligible liabilities of a bank represent its sterling deposit base, which it can employ for the purpose of holding UK assets. In practice, however, precise definitions of deposits are required and account has to be taken of some aspects of the banks' international activities. Thus the definition of eligible liabilities is as follows:

1 sterling deposits, of an original maturity of two years or under, from UK residents (other than banks) and from overseas residents;
2 sterling deposits from banks in the UK, less any sterling claims on such banks;
3 sterling certificates of deposit issued less any holdings of such certificates;
4 a bank's net deposit liability, if any, in sterling to its overseas offices;
5 all funds due to customers and third parties which are temporarily held on suspense accounts;
6 a bank's net liability, if any, in currencies other than sterling;

7 *less* 60 per cent of the net value of transit items in the bank's balance sheet.

The first category includes the great bulk of the banks' ordinary deposit liabilities, but it excludes inter-bank deposits (deposits of one UK bank with another), which are treated separately. Since banks often act as both borrowers and lenders in the inter-bank market – probably borrowing in one maturity range and lending in another – rather than having the whole of such deposits treated as an eligible liability the banks have been permitted to offset their claims on other UK banks against their deposits from them. The same treatment is applied to sterling certificates of deposit, where the banks operate as both issuers and holders of these claims. Thus for both inter-bank deposits and certificates of deposit the obligation to hold reserve assets falls upon the bank employing funds outside the banking sector, rather than merely passing them on to another bank. Funds held on suspense accounts are available for employment by the bank and are treated as deposits.

The next two items – a bank's net deposit liabilities, if any, in sterling to its overseas offices and its net liability in currencies other than sterling – both arise from the participation of UK banks in international business. The London offices of such international banks frequently act as intermediaries, for example taking deposits from a branch in one country and relending to a branch in another or holding Eurodollar deposits and making Eurodollar loans. To the extent that inward and outward flows match, the UK economy is little affected, and in each case only the net balance of liabilities is treated as an eligible liability for control purposes.

The final item, an adjustment for transit items, reflects the fact that the gross deposits of the banking system exceed their liabilities to the public, because cheques paid into accounts are credited at the time they are paid in but are not normally debited to the payer's account until two or three days later. The timing is reversed with credit transfers, where the debit takes place immediately and the credit follows later, and in addition some proportion of payments are made into accounts which are overdrawn and go therefore to reduce bank loans rather than increase bank deposits. The figure of 60 per cent of net transit items is an approximate estimate of the net effect on deposit balances.

Special deposits

The object of imposing a reserve assets ratio was to provide the authorities with a firm base for controlling monetary and credit conditions, and their intention was to use open market operations as the normal means of influencing the size of that base in the short run. But the authorities also reserved the right to require the banks to make special deposits with the Bank of England. A call for special deposits would reduce the reserve assets available to the banking system, and conversely the release of special deposits would supply additional reserves. The authorities may choose in some circumstances to employ special deposits in preference to open market operations as a means of control. Interest at the treasury bill rate is normally paid on special deposits.

The $12\frac{1}{2}$ per cent reserve assets ratio applies equally to all of the elements of eligible liabilities, but the special deposits scheme may be applied at different rates to different categories of liability. In particular the rate of call may be different for domestic and for overseas deposits in excess of those held at the time the call is made.

Non-interest-bearing supplementary special deposits can also be used as a means of enforcing guidelines given to individual banks. During several extended periods since December 1973 banks have been required to hold the growth of their interest-bearing liabilities below a defined limit, with the penalty of having to make supplementary special deposits if growth was excessive (see pages 70–77).

Institutions covered

Two groups of institutions are included within the scheme, the banks and the finance houses. These cover practically all the institutions which take large deposits, though other deposit-taking institutions, such as the building societies, are excluded. Historically, the banks and finance houses had been subject to credit controls and it was therefore natural to bring both these groups into the scheme. Since the finance houses had not been accustomed to holding any significant liquid assets, a lower ratio was specified for them, namely 10 per cent. However, subsequent to the introduction of the scheme most large finance houses opted to be treated as banks since, although their reserve asset ratio was increased, with banking status they could obtain funds more cheaply from other banks who were able to offset such loans against their own borrowing in computing their eligible liabilities.

It should, perhaps, be pointed out that the other main groups of deposit-taking institutions, the National Savings Bank, the Trustee Savings Banks and the building societies, are also subject to statutory controls on their business; and in addition they are frequently the recipients of informal government pressure. Thus, although not included within the formal credit control scheme, they are by no means entirely free to follow their own devices.

The discount market

The discount market holds a special position in the British financial system, which is reflected in the monetary control scheme. Money at call with the discount houses is counted as a reserve asset and this means that, to the extent that they are financed from money at call from the banks, the assets in the discount houses' portfolios themselves take on the character of reserve assets. Some of the assets, for example gilt-edged stocks with up to a year to maturity or treasury bills, would count as reserve assets if held directly by the banks concerned, but others, such as certificates of deposit, commercial bills or gilt-edged securities with a maturity of over one year, would not.

If the discount houses were left entirely free to expand their assets it would be possible for the banking system to manufacture reserve assets readily. For example, when reserve assets were in short supply the banks would issue additional certificates of deposit and employ some of the funds they raised as money at call with the discount market, who in turn would use this money to hold some of the newly-issued certificates. Although the return on money at call would be significantly below the yield on certificates of deposit, this would still be profitable for the banks because the balance of the funds they raised would be employed in much higher yielding assets such as advances. It must be emphasized that this process would be likely to take place without any connivance between the banks and the discount houses, because relative interest-rate movements would provide the necessary incentive to both groups of institutions.

Table 3.2 provides a schematic illustration of the mechanism of reserve asset creation. Bank deposits are divided into two categories, certificates of deposit and other deposits, and funds

Table 3.2 Reserve Asset Creation

Banks

Deposits			*Assets*		
	(a)	(b)		(a)	(b)
Certificates of deposit	10	15	Reserve assets		
Other deposits	90	90	Money at call	8	9
			Other	6	6
			Advances	60	64
			Other assets	26	26
Total deposits	100	105	Total assets	100	105

Discount Market

Liabilities			*Assets*		
	(a)	(b)		(a)	(b)
Money at call from banks	8	9	'Undefined assets'		
			Certificates of deposit	2	3
Other liabilities	2	2	Other	5	5
			Other assets	3	3
Total liabilities	10	11	Total assets	10	11

employed in reserve assets, advances and other assets. Within reserve assets, money at call with the discount market is shown separately. The discount market obtains the bulk of its resources from this source, and employs its funds in certificates of deposit and other assets. The significance of the distinction between 'undefined assets' and 'other assets' will be explained later.

The columns headed (a) show the initial situation, in which the portfolios of the banks and discount market are in equilibrium. Now suppose that the banks experience an increase in demand for advances, and being unwilling or unable to contract their 'other assets' seek to attract additional funds by issuing more certificates of deposit. We assume that the offer of a higher yield on certificates of deposit will persuade asset-holders at home or abroad to redeploy funds which would otherwise be held in other forms.

These increases in the banks' deposits create a need for additional reserve assets. They wish therefore to employ part of the new deposits in reserve assets, with the balance available to meet the demand for advances. But there is no increase in the public-sector element of the supply of reserve assets. The yield on reserve assets therefore tends to fall, as the banks bid against each other to increase their holdings, at the same time as the yield on certificates of deposit (and on bank advances) is rising. The discount houses therefore find it profitable to increase the size of their books, by buying certificates of deposit and borrowing the necessary funds from the banks. (Alternatively, they may alter the composition of their assets, buying certificates of deposit and selling reserve assets held by them to the banks).

The outcome is shown in the columns headed (b) in Table 3.2. The banks have raised an extra five of certificates of deposit, and employed four in advances and one in money at call: the yield on the extra advances is sufficient to compensate them for having to employ part of the new deposits in comparatively low-yielding call money. The banks have maintained their reserve asset ratio The discount market's holding of certificates of deposit and their borrowing from the banks have both increased by one unit.

It is important to observe that creation of private-sector reserve assets by this means involves an increase in the discount market's holding of private-sector debt (certificates of deposit). When the new scheme was first instituted, in order to limit the scope for reserve asset creation by this means, the authorities accordingly agreed with the discount houses that the latter would employ a minimum of 50 per cent of their borrowed funds in holdings of defined categories[1] of public-sector debt. This meant that a discount house whose holdings were at the minimum level had to purchase additional public-sector assets, which might well be unprofitable since such assets as treasury bills were likely to yield less than the cost of additional funds. In practice this restriction was a source of difficulty both for the discount houses and for the Bank of England in its day-to-day operation in the market.[2] So in July 1973, it was replaced by an agreement that the discount houses would not hold in their portfolios assets other than those in the previously defined categories exceeding a multiple of twenty times their free capital and reserves.[3] These assets are known as the 'undefined assets', and their ratio to free capital and reserves has been given the elegant title of the 'undefined assets multiple'. This puts an upper limit on the extent to which the banks and discount market together can provide themselves with reserve assets. It was expected initially that the limit would be reached only very occasionally by any discount house, while the multiple for the market as a whole would generally be at a considerably lower level; but this expectation has not been borne out in practice. The new rule means that when the discount houses are operating with a low multiple, e.g. at the beginning of a credit squeeze, considerable scope for expansion of reserve assets exists. But the scope is not unlimited and the authorities have at their disposal means of offsetting any

1. 'Defined assets' comprise:

1 balances at the Bank of England;
2 treasury bills;
3 gilt-edged and local authority stocks with not more than five years to maturity;
4 local authority and certain other public bodies' bills;
5 local authority negotiable bonds.

2. When the Bank of England bought in treasury bills from the discount houses to relieve a shortage of cash the houses were forced to sell private-sector assets or bid aggressively for other public-sector assets. This increased the yield margin between the two categories of asset. To avoid this the Bank of England at times bought in commercial bills when providing cash to the market, thus refinancing private-sector credit – an effect which was not always consistent with other aims of policy.

3. Calculated as a three-year moving average of end-December figures for each discount house.

additional reserve assets created, e.g. by calling for special deposits from the banks.

Bank of England operations: (i) cash

The Bank of England is responsible for ensuring that the private sector has the cash it needs, and it is able to predict quite accurately how much that will be. The net effect of payments between the central government and the Bank of England on the one hand and the remainder of the economy on the other appears as a change in the banks' deposits with the Bank of England, and the obligation on the clearing banks to adhere to a $1\frac{1}{2}$ per cent cash ratio allows the Bank to estimate the size of any shortfall or surplus. The Bank of England will always supply the cash the market needs, by lending to it or by buying in treasury bills or other short-term assets, but the Bank can choose the terms on which it is prepared to deal and so influences short-term rates of interest on reserve assets. Thus when operating in the money and treasury bill markets the Bank of England has two main objectives – to smooth out any random day-to-day unevenness in the net payments between the authorities and the private sector, and to influence the level of short-term interest rates.

The main causes of fluctuations in daily cash payments between the authorities and the private sector are connected with government expenditure and tax receipts, purchases and sales of gilt-edged securities, the supply of currency, and transactions involving foreign exchange. If the authorities took no action to offset these random fluctuations, conditions in the money market would vary sharply from shortage to surplus of funds: a net payment of, say, £100 million must be seen in relation to total bankers' deposits with the Bank of England of about £400 million. However, since payment is frequently not due until one or two days after transactions take place, and since the authorities are able to predict ahead a major part of their own spending and tax receipts, the Bank of England can generally iron out any major fluctuations if it wishes. It does this by issuing each week slightly more treasury bills than it expects to be necessary for the purpose of government financing in that week, and then buys in treasury bills from the market to supply any cash needed on a day-to-day basis. If a surplus of funds in the market arises, e.g. because of an inflow of foreign exchange, the authorities can sell additional treasury bills to absorb the surplus. These actions are carried out as a matter of routine to avoid unwanted fluctuations in the supply of funds.

By their policy of keeping cash generally tight or making it generally easy the authorities can influence the level of short-term interest rates, raising it in the former and lowering it in the latter case. They can always be sure of selling as many treasury bills at the weekly tender as they wish, since the discount houses have agreed to bid for the entire issue, which means that the authorities are usually in a strong position to create a cash squeeze, though from time to time a substantial inflow of funds from abroad could impede their actions. They are also able to provide cash to avoid a shortage or to encourage a reduction in short-term interest rates. Normally they do this by buying in treasury bills from the market, but if there is a shortage of treasury bills they may also deal in short-dated gilt-edged securities, in local authority or commercial bills, or even make short-term deposits with local authorities to offset temporary cash shortages.

When the Bank of England wants to raise short-term interest rates it either reduces the prices it is prepared to pay for assets bought in to relieve cash shortages or forces the discount houses to borrow from it. The rate charged is generally the Bank of England's minimum lending rate, which is normally a little higher than the interest rate on treasury bills. Borrowing at this rate hits discount houses' profitability directly, because it means that they must run part of their portfolio at a loss, but it is also taken as a signal that the Bank believes rates should rise and will keep cash short until they do.[1] Prices of assets therefore fall (i.e. rates of interest rise) to take account of the likelihood of tighter monetary conditions. The minimum lending rate (MLR) replaced Bank rate, which was abolished in October 1972. From then until May 1978 MLR was generally market-determined –

1. If the shortage of funds is accidental the Bank generally lends funds overnight, but if it is trying to raise interest rates it lends for a minimum of seven days, thus imposing a more severe penalty.

related by a formula to the average tender rate on treasury bills in the previous week – though the Bank of England retained and occasionally used the power to suspend the formula and change MLR autonomously. Previously changes in Bank rate had acquired a somewhat exaggerated psychological and political significance, which conflicted with the new approach to monetary control; the change to MLR helped to take routine monetary control operations out of the political arena, while by suspending the formula the authorities could still influence the climate of opinion if they wished. In May 1978, however, the Bank decided to revert to setting MLR by administrative action, on the grounds that erratic movements in the treasury bill rate occasionally gave rise to changes in MLR which were at odds with the needs of monetary policy.

Bank of England operations: (ii) reserve assets

Day-to-day fluctuations in the net payments between the authorities and the rest of the economy also affect the reserve assets of the banking system. But in this context random movements are of little importance – a fluctuation of, say, £100 million must be compared with total reserve assets held by the banks of about £6000 million: what matters is the cumulative total of these payments over a period.

We have already seen how government financing needs can influence the reserve base of the banking system, through its effect on the central bank's balance sheet. This is also true of the UK, though since government debt itself forms the predominant part of the reserve base, there is no need for intermediation by the central bank – the government simply borrows directly from the commercial banks. The UK government requires finance to cover the public sector's deficit, that is, the excess of the government's current and capital spending over its current revenue; its net lending, that is, the excess of new loans over receipts from loan repayments; and to refinance maturing debt. Funds can be obtained in several ways – by selling marketable securities, by borrowing in other forms such as non-marketable securities, by selling assets such as foreign exchange, or by borrowing from the banking system. These possibilities can be summarized in the government financing identity:[1]

$$PSD + MAT = OMO + NMD + FE + \Delta SD + \Delta H,$$

where PSD = public-sector deficit;

MAT = funds required for maturities;

OMO = outcome of open-market operations;

NMD = transactions in non-marketable debt;

FE = reduction in foreign exchange assets;

ΔSD = increase in special deposits;

ΔH = increase in public-sector's monetary liabilities.

This can be rewritten as:

$$\Delta H = PSD + MAT - OMO - NMD - FE - \Delta SD.$$

We shall examine each of these terms in turn to see to what extent the monetary authorities can expect to influence them. The public sector deficit (PSD) is the net financial outcome of government spending, lending and tax policies. Finance is required not only for the government's own current spending, but also for capital spending on basic services in the economy and for loans to help finance the capital expenditure programmes of bodies such as nationalized industries; tax receipts generally cover much of the current expenditure and probably some of the capital expenditure too, but there is no reason why receipts and expenditure should balance exactly. Government policies, both for expenditure and receipts, have some regard to the capacity of the economy to provide loan finance, but they are much more strongly influenced by the political and economic objectives of the government of the day. While spending and taxation are always subject to unplanned changes, due to the effects of inflation, shortages etc., discretionary changes are infrequent and usually take place in the context of reviews of government policy. Moreover, when discretionary changes are made they are often determined largely by non-monetary considerations.

Maturities of existing securities (MAT) add to the government's

1. The approach employed here follows Goodhart (1972).

need for funds and are another cause of new loan issues. Government debt management operations are usually carried out almost continuously to maintain the maturity of outstanding debt: otherwise, as each day passed, the average maturity would shorten. In Britain the authorities make a practice of buying in before the actual maturity date issues which will mature in the near future and selling simultaneously longer dated stocks. Since many holders of debt are also concerned to maintain the average maturity of their holdings, the wishes of the authorities frequently coincide with those of security holders. However it is by no means always so, particularly where a security has been held very widely by the general public, and the holders of maturing stock may be very reluctant to reinvest their funds. The occasion of a maturity causes such holders to review their portfolio, and money which is received may go into goods or other financial assets rather than be reinvested in government stock.

The public are also able to subscribe for non-marketable government securities (*NMD*), consisting mainly of the category of assets known as national savings. A feature of these debt instruments is that the rates of interest offered are usually sticky. With some forms of national savings the monetary authorities in Britain try to keep the interest return (after allowing for tax concessions) broadly in line with the general level of interest rates, and are unwilling to alter interest rates frequently; it is therefore easy for rates to depart temporarily from the general level. (In contrast, the yields offered on local authority mortgages – also non-marketable debt – react quickly to other interest rate movements.) In consequence the net inflow of funds into national savings securities tends to move inversely with market rates of interest. While the monetary authorities do influence the yields offered on non-marketable securities in the long run, the finance raised from this source is outside their control in the short run.

As we have already seen, the banking system's reserve base is affected by changes in a country's gold and foreign exchange reserves. In the UK the government holds the reserves in a special account (the Exchange Equalization Account), so it is the government's own borrowing rather than that of the Bank of England which is affected by foreign exchange flows. When there is a balance of payments deficit the private sector buys foreign exchange from the authorities to pay for its net imports. The government's need to borrow is therefore reduced to the extent that it raises funds by selling an asset, foreign exchange (FE); conversely, if there is a balance of payments surplus the government needs to borrow more in order to pay for the foreign exchange it acquires. The underlying balance of payments position on current account is something which the authorities cannot alter quickly, but by influencing domestic interest rates they can encourage or discourage capital flows from abroad which affect the foreign exchange reserves and the government's need to borrow at home.

In Britain open-market operations (OMO) in government securities cannot be distinguished from government debt management in general. They are concerned, not with changing the liabilities of the Bank of England, but with altering the maturity structure of government debt, so that the amount qualifying as reserve assets is controlled. The Bank of England's dealing practices in different categories of gilt-edged securities reflect their status as reserve or non-reserve assets. As already mentioned the Bank of England makes a practice of buying in gilt-edged stocks before maturity, and when a stock is within one year of maturity the Bank stands ready to buy any stock offered to it, thus adding to the cash resources in the market. This provides the rationale for including gilt-edged stocks with less than one year to maturity in reserve assets, because their purchase by the Bank changes the composition of reserve assets but not their total.

Bank of England purchases or sales of longer-dated gilt-edged securities do affect reserve assets as a whole. The Bank of England is now prepared to buy longer-dated gilt-edged securities only at its discretion, and will not automatically accept any block of stock offered to it. The same generally applies to sales of stocks from its own portfolio. To facilitate the refinancing of the debt the Bank of England is also prepared to exchange stock, at prices of its own choosing, with the market with the object of maintaining or lengthening the average maturity of the debt ('funding'). Thus it will generally be prepared to exchange a long-dated stock from its own portfolio for a shorter-dated stock on offer in the market. By this means it assists asset holders, such as pension funds, who wish to maintain the average maturity of their own government debt holdings.

It should be noted that these dealing practices represent a departure from what prevailed in the ten years or so before May 1971. In that period the Bank of England was generally prepared to accept, at a price not very different from the ruling market price, any stock offered by the market, with the result that control over the volume of liquid assets in the banking system was effectively lost. Now, unless very large sums have to be found to finance a government deficit (or a balance of payments surplus) the Bank holds the initiative in determining the supply of reserve assets.

Open-market operations are carried out almost continuously, and are the normal means of making relatively small adjustments in the volume of reserve assets. Needless to say, if open-market sales (or purchases) are carried out consistently over a period of weeks or months the total effect can be substantial. Nevertheless, in some circumstances conventional open-market operations may not be a good, or even feasible, means of controlling the money supply and the volume of reserve assets. If, for example, a substantial public sector borrowing requirement is feeding both the money supply and the banks' reserve asset holdings, the authorities may from time to time have difficulty in selling enough gilt-edged securities. When conditions are unsettled the financial institutions' and general public's appetite for gilt-edged stocks is usually poor, and to attract enough buyers the authorities might have to offer very high yields – much higher than would be required to sell the same amount of stock when more settled conditions returned. In conditions like this special deposits may be superior to open-market operations as an instrument for mopping up the excess liquidity flowing into the system.

If, in response to a credit squeeze, the private sector is creating reserve assets by borrowing from abroad, these too may be mopped up by special deposits. Indeed, the possibility that funds might flow in from overseas, and thereby offset credit restraint, led the authorities to incorporate in the control scheme the arrangements by which special deposits at a differential rate might be called against the banks' net liabilities to overseas residents, whether in sterling or other currencies. To avoid unfairness any differential call for special deposits would be on the margin of such liabilities over what had existed at a base date. The object would be to discourage an inflow of funds from abroad by ensuring that part of it – a larger part than normal – would be invested in a relatively low-yielding form. This provision has not yet (June 1979) been used in practice.

A release of special deposits might be expected in circumstances which are the reverse of those leading to a call, i.e. when a shortage of reserve assets threatens to squeeze credit unduly the authorities can be expected to release special deposits as and when the opportunity arises. On several occasions the authorities have in fact released special deposits temporarily when very large sales of gilt-edged securities or a foreign exchange outflow threatened to drain too much liquidity from the banking system.

The ability of the banking system in the UK to manufacture its own reserve assets, by increasing the volume of commercial bills in the banks' portfolios (up to the 2 per cent limit) or basing money at call on non-reserve assets, complicates the Bank of England's task in controlling the volume of reserve assets. When the authorities are trying to tighten credit conditions by reducing treasury bills and short-dated gilt-edged stocks they may find their efforts to control the reserve base partially or wholly offset by an expansion – though not without limit – of these other reserve assets. And, no doubt, if at other times the authorities wished to expand credit their efforts might also be frustrated.

Finally we must note that in the UK, in common with other countries, the prescribed reserve asset ratio is a minimum. Typically the banks hold excess reserves, and the size of the excess will reflect the relative interest rates on reserve and non-reserve assets. During a credit squeeze this margin widens and the banks are content to work with reserve ratios closer to the minimum. The Bank of England has to cope with this contraction in the demand for reserve assets, and consequently cut the supply by more than would otherwise be necessary.

Monetary control in practice

The present scheme for controlling the money supply in the United Kingdom has now been in operation for nearly eight years. During this period it has undergone several modifications, some of which amount to significant changes in the character of the scheme itself. The Supplementary Special Deposits scheme was introduced in December 1973, and since the middle of 1976 the authorities have been setting target ranges for the growth of M_3.

Table 3.3 The UK Money Supply

		M_1 £ million	Sterling M_3 £ million			M_1 £ million	Sterling M_3 £ million
1972	1	11,180⎫ 11,240⎭	20,630⎫ 21,040⎭	1976	1	17,920	37,670
	2	11,670	22,490		2	18,310	38,650
	3	11,860	23,460		3	19,190	40,300
	4	12,320	24,890		4	19,150	40,570
				1977	1	19,750	40,800
1973	1	12,330	26,330⎫ 26,240⎭		2	20,470	41,900
	2	13,120	27,650		3	21,820	42,710
	3	12,750	29,730		4	23,330	44,660
	4	13,120	31,610	1978	1	24,250	46,700
					2	24,620	48,010
1974	1	12,750	32,450		3	25,790	49,170
	2	13,100	32,680		4	27,190	51,370
	3	13,530	33,520				
	4	14,550	34,840				
1975	1	14,830	35,210				
	2	15,170⎫ 15,900⎭	35,730⎫ 35,710⎭				
	3	16,730	36,900				
	4	17,340	37,200				

Source: *Financial Statistics*, April 1979 and earlier editions.

The growth of the money supply (M_1 and Sterling M_3) in the years 1972 to 1978 is shown in Table 3.3 and Figure 3.1. On both measures money grew by about 150 per cent over the whole period, but the pattern of growth differed. At first the growth of M_3, which is directly related to the banks' reserve base, was very rapid; indeed, during 1972 and 1973 it averaged about 25 per cent per year. The rate of growth was halved in 1974, and fell to under 8 per cent in 1975 before picking up again during 1976. Measures to curb the rate of growth were taken at the end of the year and were successful, but more rapid expansion followed and M_3 grew by 15 per cent in 1978. Private lending was the dominant expansionary influence for most of the period, but from 1974 on the funding of a very large public-sector borrowing requirement, without excessive recourse to the banking system, was a major preoccupation of the authorities. The growth of M_1 was much more erratic. It appears to have been influenced quite strongly by changes in interest rates as well as by the rise in money incomes; high rates of interest on deposit accounts in 1973 and again at the end of 1976 encouraged switching from current to deposit accounts, with some reversal as interest rates fell subsequently. Four sub-periods can be distinguished. Monetary growth was

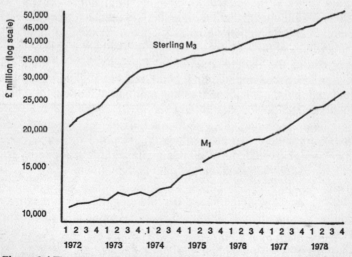

Figure 3.1 The UK money supply

extremely rapid from September 1971, when the new scheme was introduced, to December 1973. At first this was fully in accord with the authorities' wishes; in the autumn of 1971 the stance of monetary policy was expansionary since output was running well below capacity and unemployment was growing. But in the middle of 1972 the authorities became concerned about the rapid increase in the money stock and began to take measures designed to restrain its growth. From then on the stance of monetary policy was generally restrictive. Yet Figure 3.1 shows that it was not until 1974 that monetary expansion really began to moderate. Why did it take so long for a more restrictive policy to have a discernible effect on the rate of monetary growth?

There are a number of reasons why the Bank of England failed to act with sufficient resolution at this time. It was difficult to be sure what was going on. M_3 and M_1 were telling different stories about monetary growth; teething troubles connected with the new system made it likely that M_3 exaggerated the underlying rate of monetary growth; and, with their new freedom to compete, the banks were in any case expected to grow at the expense of other financial intermediaries. In addition, there was a great deal of slack in the system, which made it difficult to control. As Table 3.4 shows, the banks' reserve asset ratio fell from over 17 per cent at the end of 1971 to 13·8 per cent at the end of 1973 – sufficient to allow an increase of over 25 per cent in M_3 without any rise in the reserve asset base. Furthermore, the discount houses' public-sector lending ratio fell, and when this was replaced by the undefined assets multiple there was a sharp increase from just under 14 to over 17 by the end of the year. The banks' holdings of commercial bills as reserve assets also rose from under 1 per cent to nearly 2 per cent of their eligible liabilities. This added up to a very substantial increase in the volume of reserve assets, created in effect by the banking system itself.

While the new system relied on interest rates as the means of controlling monetary expansion, Bank rate was still a sensitive political issue. In June 1972 there was a foreign exchange crisis during which Bank rate was raised to 6 per cent – the banks were given only short-term assistance to counteract the sudden drain

Table 3.4 Monetary Control Statistics

	Banks' Reserve Assets Ratio	Discount Market's Undefined Assets Multiple*	MLR	Special Deposits
	(%)		(%)	(%)
December 1971	17·4	(65·8%)	5	NIL
June 1972	14·5	(59·3%)	6	NIL
December 1972	15·7	(57.2%)	9	1
June 1973	14.2	(54.2%)	7½	3
December 1973	13.8	17.5	13	5
June 1974	13·5	18.8	11¾	3
December 1974	13.6	19.4	11½	3
June 1975	14.6	18.6	10	3
December 1975	15·1	15·3	11¼	3
June 1976	15·2	13·9	11½	3
December 1976	13·8	16·8	14¼	5
June 1977	14·0	14·0	8	3
December 1977	14·8	16·0	7	3
June 1978	13·8	18.3	10	1½
December 1978	13·6	17·9	12¼	3

* Public-Sector Lending Ratio until June 1973

Source: *Financial Statistics*, April 1979 and earlier editions.

on their liquidity – but a further rise had to await the change to MLR in October. Interest rates rose again by the end of the year, but eased in the first half of 1973. In July, prompted by the deteriorating exchange rate and rising interest rates abroad, the Bank created a liquidity squeeze by calling for special deposits and MLR rose from 7½ per cent, first to 9 per cent and then to 11½ per cent in line with changes in the tender rates for treasury bills. But an interest ceiling of 9½ per cent on retail bank deposits was imposed, to prevent a rise in building society mortgage rates. In November the squeeze was intensified when the Bank called for a further 2 per cent of special deposits (1 per cent of which was cancelled subsequently) and raised MLR by administrative action to 13 per cent.

Creating a reserve asset squeeze and thus forcing up interest rates was one function of special deposits in this period. But they were also used for another purpose: when late in 1972 and in 1973 government borrowing from the banking system took place, special deposits (amounting to 3 per cent in all) were called to prevent this leading to an increase in reserve assets.

The introduction of the Supplementary Special Deposits scheme in December 1973, which placed a limit on the growth of banks' interest-bearing sterling liabilities, can be regarded as a major modification of the control system. The aim was to deter banks from bidding actively for deposits as a means of avoiding the reserve assets squeeze. The obligation to make non-interest-bearing special deposits with the Bank of England, if they exceeded the stipulated growth in their deposits, made excess growth prohibitively expensive. The scheme came to be known as 'the corset' because it served to constrict each bank's activities. Like the advances ceilings of the 1960s, the corset inhibits competition between banks, reduces the upward pressure on deposit interest rates, and encourages credit flows which bypass the banking system.

The second sub-period runs from the beginning of 1974 until the autumn of 1976. The measures taken at the end of the previous year to slow down monetary growth were effective, but the sharp worsening of the economic climate, both at home and abroad, led to an even faster reduction in the demand for credit. The Bank was therefore able to release 2 per cent of special deposits within a few months, and interest rates declined gradually until the spring of 1975. The banks' reserve asset ratios also rose. The corset gradually became redundant and was removed in February 1975. Higher interest rates abroad and weakening of the exchange rate caused MLR to rise in the summer, but the downward trend was resumed later in the year, and continued in the first quarter of 1976.

At that time the authorities were concerned that the sterling exchange rate was too high, and would damage the international competitiveness of UK products. They therefore actively sought a decline in short-term interest rates, with a view to encouraging an outflow of short-term funds which would tend to weaken the exchange rate. Sterling fell sharply – much faster than the authorities had intended – and at the same time monetary growth accelerated. The banking system was liquid, with little pressure on reserve assets to discourage an expansion of bank lending. Although after a fall of some 10 per cent the exchange rate held stable through most of the summer, aided by a rise in interest rates, it began to fall again in September. The treasury bill rate and MLR rose, followed by a call for 1 per cent of special deposits in September. In July the Chancellor of the Exchequer had announced a target rate of growth for the money supply of 12 per cent for the year, but by October money was clearly growing much too fast – 9 per cent in six months. The Bank therefore raised MLR by 2 per cent to 15 per cent, reiterated the 12 per cent guideline for monetary growth and made a further call for 2 per cent of special deposits (1 per cent of which was subsequently cancelled); this removed much of the banks' spare liquidity. Nevertheless, when in November the money supply still seemed to be growing strongly the authorities reintroduced the corset scheme. For the second time direct controls on individual banks were used instead of even higher interest rates to bring about a quick change of trend. In December the government announced measures in connection with a loan from the International Monetary Fund, including a limit on credit expansion which implied that the growth of Sterling M_3 in 1977/78 should lie between 9 per cent and 13 per cent.

The third sub-period runs from the end of 1976 to October 1977. Confidence in sterling had been restored by the IMF loan and associated measures, and the authorities attempted to stabilize the exchange rate. This led to a massive inflow of funds from abroad. To discourage this inflow MLR was allowed to decline, and fell to 5 per cent by October; 2 per cent of special deposits were released early in the year; and the corset, which had the desired effect in curtailing monetary growth, was suspended in August. By the autumn, however, liquidity in the banking system was building up and monetary growth had begun to accelerate. The authorities were therefore compelled to choose between holding down the exchange rate and attempting to adhere to their monetary target; they chose the latter, and allowed both the exchange rate and MLR to rise. In spite of this M_3 overshot the target range significantly in 1977/78.

The final period runs from the end of 1977. The authorities have aimed to check the growth of M_3 within target ranges – 9 per cent to 13 per cent for 1977/78 and 8 per cent to 12 per cent subsequently. Special deposits have been held at a basic level of 3 per cent, with several temporary reductions to ease temporary liquidity shortages in the banking system. The automatic link between MLR and the treasury bill rate was removed in May. MLR rose to 10 per cent in June 1978, and with the banking system's liquidity under pressure and the discount market unable to increase the supply of reserve assets, the Bank of England re-activated the corset. Short-term rates rose further in the early autumn, and for a period treasury bill rate lay above MLR; this was therefore raised to $12\frac{1}{2}$ per cent in November. There was a further rise to 14 per cent in February 1979. As usual the corset diverted some credit flows away from the banking system, which helped to keep the growth of M_3 in 1978/79 just within the target range.

To sum up, the monetary control system in the UK now places considerable emphasis on a target range for the rate of growth of M_3; this range is set for a period of twelve months ahead and revised every six months. The authorities attempt through their interest rate policy to keep monetary growth within this range, and they try to ensure that the reserve assets of the banking system are consistent with this. From time to time a change in MLR or reserve asset pressure is employed to effect the changes in short-term interest rates which the authorities believe to be necessary. Special deposits have been used flexibly to maintain the intended degree of pressure on reserve assets. But the authorities do not rely entirely on interest rates and reserve assets. The corset has been imposed on three occasions, and has in fact (in June 1979) been in force for about 60 per cent of the time since its introduction in December 1973.

The last eight years have been characterized by a quite remarkable degree of interest rate volatility. In part this is a consequence of the exceptional instability in economic affairs, but in part it may also be a consequence of the way in which monetary policy has been conducted. For example, in both 1975 and 1977 liquidity was allowed to build up within the banking system (as well as outside), rendering much more difficult the task of slowing down monetary growth afterwards. Not only has this led to high interest rates, it has also compelled the authorities to resort to the corset. Smoother monetary control in future may entail keeping closer control of liquidity at times of expansion, and a willingness by the authorities to subordinate other objectives to the requirements of monetary policy.

4 The Demand for Money: Theory

Introduction

For well over two hundred years in economic literature the quantity of money has been singled out for special attention, reflecting the common belief that money, prices and economic activity are in some way linked. Theories have varied from the supposition that a rigid relation existed between the quantity of money and the value of transactions which it could support – as if money were an intermediate product employed with a fixed technical coefficient in the production of final output – through the hypothesis that the level of money income was the dominant, though not the sole, influence on the quantity of money required, to the belief that money is best regarded as one amongst a number of alternative ways of holding wealth and that its demand is determined by its relative yield and other attributes. The fixed technical coefficient theory is the basis of the most rigid version of the quantity theory of money; the income theory lies behind the less rigid 'Cambridge' version of this theory – which was elaborated and extended by Keynes – and the asset theory is the foundation of the modern quantity theory of money.

Before considering each of these approaches in turn we should note that all seek to explain the equilibrium demand for money, and that in reality the quantity of money actually held in a community subject to change is very likely to differ from the long-term equilibrium level which might be expected in a stationary state. Since money is the medium of exchange any temporary imbalance between an individual's income and expenditure is reflected in a change in his money balance, to which he reacts subsequently by purchasing or selling financial assets or adjusting his income and expenditure flows. The process of adjustment is by no means instantaneous and there is a time-lag of uncertain length before equilibrium is reached. The same applies to reactions to any changes in financial conditions which affect the demand for money. What is true of the individual holds also in this instance for the community as a whole: any imbalance between borrower's demands and the supply of savings available shows up initially as a temporary expansion or contraction of short-term credit, which is reflected in the quantity of money.[1]

Most of the earlier empirical studies of the demand for money employed annual data and treated the quantity of money in existence as the equilibrium amount, on the assumption that the time required for adjustment in the system was small in relation to the interval between successive observations on the money stock. However, for more recent studies employing quarterly data it has been usual to construct dynamic models in which the short-term equilibrium at the end of each quarter reflects only a partial adjustment towards the long-term equilibrium which the system would ultimately reach.

The quantity theory approach

The notion that the quantity of money is linked rigidly to the value of transactions lies behind one version of the quantity theory of money. Irving Fisher (1911) developed the well-known quantity equation:

$$MV \equiv PT,$$

where M is the quantity of money, V is the transactions-velocity of circulation, P is the price level and T the volume of transactions.

In itself this is not a *theory* of the demand for money; rather given empirical measures of M, P and T it is an *identity* which defines the value of V. However, with the aid of three hypotheses about economic behaviour it can be turned into a theory of the determination of the price level. Suppose M is determined exogenously, V is a constant, T is determined by the full-employment output of the economy. Then

$$P = \frac{V}{T}M$$

1. In the short term banks generally try to accommodate their customers' needs for credit, and tolerate any changes in their reserve positions which this may entail.

and any change in M is reflected in a proportional change in P.

The assumptions that M would be determined exogenously and that the economy would be in equilibrium at full employment were common classical assumptions, but the constancy of V requires more explanation. It reflected the view that given the structure of industry, the mechanism of payment and the payments practices of the community, a certain amount of money was needed to allow any given level of transactions to take place freely. Just as a fixed amount of some raw material may be required for every unit made of some product – there is a fixed technical coefficient in the production process – so a fixed amount of money was required for each unit of transactions. The technical coefficient would change if payments practices, the degree of industrial integration or other structural characteristics of the economy altered, but since, at least in the short term, all these features could be regarded as fixed the technical coefficient could also be treated as constant. This meant, for example, that it would not be affected by the cyclical behaviour of the economy. In the longer term, of course, there might be trend changes in structure which would affect the value of the technical coefficient. $1/V (= M/PT)$ measured the amount of money required per unit of transactions, and its inverse V measured the rate of turnover of each unit of money per period.

Notice that in this formulation of the quantity equation the price level must refer to all the transactions which take place, and must include purely financial transactions as well as the purchase and sale of goods and services. In order to relate the theory to the level of income, the assumption that total transactions vary directly with income must be made and the price level is then defined to refer to the price of real output. The quantity equation becomes:

$$MV = PY,$$

where Y is real income and V is now the *income*-velocity of circulation. From this equation we can deduce that the quantity of money demanded (required) for any level of income Y and prices P will be:

$$M = \frac{1}{V}PY,$$

where V is a constant.

This is the simple quantity theory of the demand for money: the demand for money varies directly with the money value of income, with the factor of proportionality $1/V$ determined by technical factors associated with the structure of the economy. This theory predicts that M will vary directly with PY without additional complicating factors. Because of this simple and unambiguous prediction it is an attractive theory, but unfortunately it is not fully supported by the facts; empirical evidence has shown that V is not constant in the short run. Nevertheless, the proposition that large changes in M are generally associated with roughly proportional changes in PY is substantially correct.

An alternative approach to the quantity theory – the 'Cambridge equation' – was developed by Cambridge economists, such as Marshall (1923) and Pigou (1917). Formally, the Cambridge equation is identical with the income version of Fisher's equation:

$$M = kPY,$$

where $k = 1/V$ in the Fisher equation. But the approach was different, in that while the Cambridge school emphasized the importance of income as a determinant of the demand for money they took the view that other factors, such as the rate of interest, might also be important. Thus k in the Cambridge equation would be constant only if other things – including the rate of interest – were constant. To avoid confusion it would have been better if this had been shown explicitly by writing:

$$M = k(r)PY,$$

where r is the rate of interest, because the omission of r from the formal equation made it all too easy to argue as if k were a constant. Before Keynes there was little attempt to analyse the nature of the dependence of k on the rate of interest.

The Keynesian approach

Keynes's (1936) contribution to the theory of the demand for money was a detailed analysis of the factors which influence demand. This analysis served to draw attention away from money income and concentrate instead on the part played by the rate of interest.

Keynes distinguished three motives for holding money. The *transactions-motive* reflected 'the need for cash for the current transaction of personal and business exchanges'; the *precautionary-motive* related to 'the desire for security as to the future cash equivalent of a certain proportion of total resources'; and the *speculative-motive* was defined as 'the object of securing profit from knowing better than the market what the future will bring forth'. Corresponding to each motive was a demand for some amount of money.

The transactions demand for money – stemming from the transactions-motive – came closest to the fixed technical co-efficient view. Money was required to bridge the intervals between the receipt and disbursement of income and between incurring of costs and receipt of sales proceeds. The amount of money required for this purpose might be expected to vary directly with the level of income. It would not, however, be unaffected by other factors such as the rate of interest, although other factors might be much less important than income. For example, when interest rates are high it may be worthwhile putting up with some inconvenience from economizing on money for the sake of the interest which could be earned by investing temporarily.[1]

The precautionary-motive is something of a hybrid. Precautionary balances are needed to provide for contingencies requiring sudden expenditure, for unforeseen opportunities of advantageous purchases, and as an asset which has a fixed money value in order to meet a subsequent liability of fixed monetary

1. On certain simplifying assumptions it can be shown that in order to maximize income the amount of money held should vary inversely with the square root of the rate of interest which could be earned if the money were invested in some other asset; see Baumol (1952) or Johnson (1967).

value. The size of the balances held for these reasons is likely also to be influenced by the level of income, but much more important determinants may well be the cost and reliability of methods of obtaining short-term credit or of encashing other assets. However, these balances are usually treated as if they moved in line with transactions balances, and are aggregated with them to form M_T – *active* balances. The relation between M_T and PY is shown as a straight line, though the slope of the line may vary with r. In Figure 4.1, r_1 measures a higher rate of interest than r_0, so M_T is lower for any value of PY.

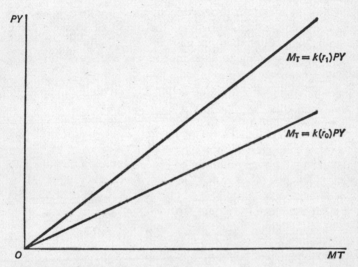

Figure 4.1 The demand for active balances

In considering the speculative demand for money Keynes focused on two alternative ways of holding financial assets, money and long-term bonds. The monetary value of the former was fixed, but that of the latter would change if the rate of interest altered. A rise in the rate of interest ruling in the market would be associated with a fall in the price of bonds which promised a fixed amount of interest annually, and vice versa if the market rate of interest fell. In deciding whether to hold money or bonds, investors would take account of the prospective capital gain or loss from holding bonds as well as the interest they would receive. It would be profitable to hold bonds rather than money provided that their capital value was not expected to fall so much as to offset the interest receivable; otherwise money, even with zero yield, should be held.

Since future interest rates are uncertain, asset-holders' expectations of how they will move are very likely to differ: some might expect interest rates to rise sharply, others might expect little change, and still others might expect a fall. All of the first group would anticipate substantial capital losses if they held bonds: they would certainly choose to hold cash. So might some of the second group, but the remainder who expected only a small capital loss on bonds – insufficient to offset the interest they would receive – and all of the third group would hold bonds. The divergence of view is thus associated with a division of asset-holders into bond-holders and money-holders, the size of these groups depending on whether general opinion expects interest rates to rise or fall. If the majority of investors[1] expect interest rates to fall the demand for bonds will be large and for money small, and vice-versa if interest rates are generally expected to rise.

In this theory 'what matters is not the *absolute* level of r, but the degree of divergence from what is considered a fairly *safe* level of r'. Individuals' views about the rate of interest are likely to be dispersed about some norm ρ. The higher is the current rate r in relation to the norm, the larger the proportion of asset-holders who will expect r to fall and so choose to hold bonds, and when r is low in relation to the norm the proportion of asset-holders who choose to hold money will be high. The relation showing the demand for speculative balances[2] M_L is known as the liquidity-preference curve. The norm itself may change, and Figure 4.2 shows two examples of liquidity preference curves, corresponding to two values of ρ. In this Figure ρ_1 is assumed to be greater than ρ_0.

1. Strictly, each investor must be given a weight equal to the value of his asset portfolio.
2. Or *idle* balances.

The speculative demand for money is thus a declining function of $r-\rho$:

$M_L = f(r-\rho)$, where $f'(r-\rho) < 0$.

Keynesians have argued further that at some positive rate of interest the elasticity of the liquidity preference curve would become infinite:[1] people would not believe that a low rate of

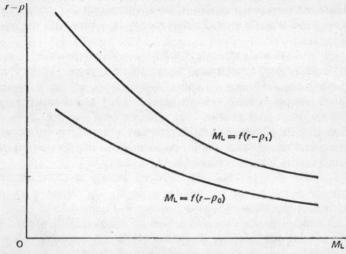

Figure 4.2 The speculative demand for money

interest would persist, and would not be compensated for the risk of capital loss by the small yield. Rather than hold bonds at a lower yield they would convert their assets into money. This part of the liquidity preference curve is known as the *liquidity trap*. Whether this occurs or not at any rate of interest which is relevant in practice is an empirical matter.

In much subsequent work the value of ρ has been treated as a constant – Keynes did not give any model for the determination of the norm – and this simplified the speculative demand for money to:

$M_L = f(r)$.

1. Leijonhufvud (1968) points out that Keynes himself did not make this assertion.

Keynes's analysis has been criticized because it assumes that apart from transactions and precautionary balances each individual holds either money or bonds but not both. The speculative demand for money increases as the proportion of investors in the money-holding category rises and that in the bond-holding category falls. This complete shift by the individual investor from one category to the other seems implausible, and Tobin (1958) has provided a model which predicts that the proportion of *each* individual's assets held as money may vary with the rate of interest.

While Keynes's explanation of liquidity preference is based on *expectations* concerning future interest rates, Tobin's is founded on *uncertainty*. Because investors are uncertain about future interest rates, bonds are seen as risky assets which may give rise to capital gain or loss, whereas cash balances have a fixed monetary value. Considering an investor's portfolio of bonds and money as a whole, an increase in the proportion of bonds carries both more income and more risk.

Suppose that in choosing between money and bonds an investor seeks income but dislikes risk. We can define a set of preference functions such as are shown in Figure 4.3.

If μ measures the expected return on the portfolio and σ its risk the investor requires more income to compensate for any increase in risk: the preference functions therefore slope upwards to the right. If it is assumed further that investors become increasingly reluctant to accept additional risk as the risk of their portfolio increases the preference curves will be convex downwards. In Figure 4.3 the curves are numbered in ascending order of preference.

Given the rate of interest on bonds, r, the opportunities open to the investor with a given amount of funds can be represented by a straight line through the origin, such as OX_1 in Figure 4.4.

At 0 the portfolio is held entirely as money – there is no income and no risk; at X_1 it is entirely in bonds, and income and risk are both maximized; as the proportion of bonds rises from zero to 100 per cent the investor moves along OX_1. With this opportunity line the highest attainable preference curve is I_2I_2, and the investor's equilibrium position will be P_1 where his portfolio

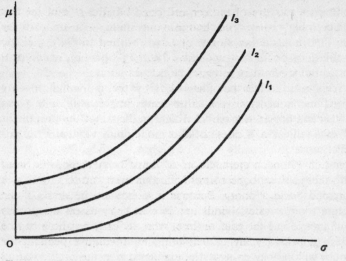

Figure 4.3 Income-risk preference functions

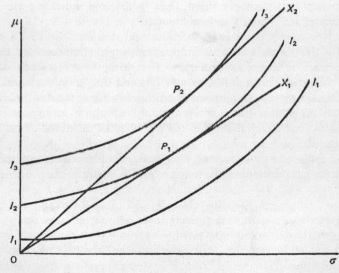

Figure 4.4 Portfolio choice

contains a mixture of money and bonds. If the rate of interest had been higher – with no change in uncertainty – the opportunity line for the same investor would have shifted to OX_2, and the equilibrium position would have been P_2 where a greater proportion of the portfolio would be held as bonds.

We should notice that this analysis explains why uncertainty might lead some investors to diversify their portfolios between money and bonds, and why a change in the rate of interest might affect the division. It does not allow us to predict that all investors will choose to diversify their portfolios – different assumptions about investors' preferences could have been made, and even with these assumptions corner solutions may lead to single-asset portfolios; and it does not allow us to predict the shape of the liquidity preference schedule, since that depends on the precise configuration of the preference curves, about which little can be said *a priori*.[1] The hypothesis that the speculative demand for money will vary inversely with the interest rate must still be based upon the Keynesian analysis of expectations.

Combining the transactions, precautionary and speculative motives for holding money gives a demand function which includes PY, r and ρ as arguments:[2]

$M = g(PY,r,\rho)$. Two further comments on this approach to the demand for money are necessary. First, if the Keynesian analysis is accepted the stability of the demand for money depends critically on the stability or predictability of ρ, the 'norm'. If investors change their opinion of what is normal in an unpredictable or erratic way, these changes will be reflected in the demand schedule, and monetary controls will be unreliable instruments for influencing the economy. The demand schedule becomes particularly unstable if the norm moves violently in the short run

1. A rise in the rate of interest would allow investors who aimed to achieve a target level of income at minimum risk to reduce their bond-holdings.

2. In the standard textbook Keynesian model it is usually assumed that the speculative demand is also proportional to prices and that p is a constant, thus simplifying the function to:

$$\frac{M}{P} = g(Y,r).$$

because investors base their expectations on an extrapolation of the recent trend in interest rates.

Secondly, in discussing the composition of wealth-holdings it seems rather odd nowadays to place so much weight on the choice between money and bonds. In most countries there are good substitutes for money which have a fixed monetary value and which often bear a higher rate of interest. It is possible that expectations about future interest rates may influence the choice between these assets and bonds rather than between money and bonds, so the speculative demand for money itself may be quantitatively rather unimportant.[1] However, the yield on these money-substitutes may have a substantial effect on the transactions demand for money.

The modern quantity theory

Modern quantity theorists treat the demand for money in just the same way as the demand for any other financial or physical asset. In consumption theory the demand for a good is determined by its attributes including its price in relation to other goods, the purchaser's set of choices being subject to an income constraint. Similarly in asset theory the demand for any particular asset is determined by its characteristics including its yield in relation to that of other assets, the asset-holder's set of choices being subject to a wealth constraint. In any empirical study of the demand for a consumption good or for a financial asset it is necessary to select from the entire range of alternatives a small number which will be treated explicitly; summary measures of relative prices or yields are needed; and the precise nature of the income or wealth constraint must be specified in some detail. The problems encountered in specifying demand functions for financial assets, including money, are no different in their essentials from the problems of consumer-demand analysis.

Friedman (1956) argues that money can be regarded as one of five broad ways of holding wealth: money, bonds, equities,

1. Leijonhufvud (1968) claims that in his discussion of the speculative demand Keynes included close substitutes along with money, and was concerned with the choice between this category of assets and those whose capital value was variable.

physical goods and human wealth. Each of these has distinctive characteristics and each offers some return in money or in kind.

The yield on money is mainly in kind – a convenience yield which reflects trouble and often costs which can be avoided if ready money is available – though as we have seen some forms of money, e.g. savings deposits in banks, also have an explicit money yield. The *real*, as opposed to nominal, yield on money depends on movements in the price level. If the price level falls, money appreciates and shows a capital gain in real terms which must be added to the nominal yield, while in the more common condition of rising prices a real capital loss has to be deducted from the nominal yield.

Bonds stand for assets which promise a perpetual income stream of constant amount. Like money, their real return is affected by changes in the price level, but it is also affected by changes in the rate of interest on bonds. If the rate of interest on bonds is r_b, the nominal rate of return can be approximated by $r_b - (1/r_b)dr_b/dt$, where $(1/r_b)dr_b/dt$ measures the rate of capital appreciation due to changes in the rate of interest.

Equities stand for assets which promise a perpetual income stream of constant real amount. If the rate of interest on equities is r_e, i.e. £1 of equities can be expected to yield annually the sum of £r_e if prices are stable, the nominal rate of return is affected both by changes in this rate of interest and by changes in the price level. The associated changes in capital value can be approximated by $-(1/r_e)dr_e/dt$ and $(1/P)dP/dt$ respectively, so the nominal rate of return must also take account of the price level P.

Physical goods yield an income in kind which can seldom be measured by any explicit rate of interest. Their nominal rate of return is, however, also affected by the rate of change of the price level $(1/P)dP/dt$ which can be considered explicitly. Human wealth is the discounted value of the expected stream of earned income. It presents a problem because it can be substituted only to a very limited extent with other forms of asset holding. Nevertheless some substitution is possible: people can sell assets in order to pay for training which will increase their future earnings, and their expected earnings also influence the amount which they can borrow and hence their gross asset holdings. In principle the limitations on substitutability make a case for distinguishing between human and non-human wealth in the demand function, which can be done by including in it the ratio of non-human to human wealth, w.

Finally, the wealth constraint must enter the demand function. In the absence of direct estimates of wealth, including human wealth, an indirect estimate must be used. Friedman makes use of *permanent income* Y_p – a weighted average of current and past values of income – as an indicator.[1] Some other investigators have confined the constraint to non-human wealth, W.

This adds up to a formidable list of factors which should enter into the demand function for money:

$$P, r_b - \frac{1}{r_b}\frac{dr_b}{dt}, r_e + \frac{1}{P}\frac{dP}{dt} - \frac{1}{r_e}\frac{dr_e}{dt}, \frac{1}{P}\frac{dP}{dt}, w \text{ and } Y_p \text{ or } W.$$

There will also, of course, be differences in individual demand functions due to differences in preferences, u.

For empirical work further simplifications must be made. First, referring back to the Keynesian analysis of the speculative demand for money, we should note that the relevant capital gains on bonds and equities are not simply those which take place in practice but those which are *expected* to take place. No measures of expected capital gains or losses due to changes in interest rates are available, so these terms are usually dropped from the demand function. The rate of change of prices has also usually been omitted, except in conditions of rapid inflation, and the ratio of non-human to human wealth has seldom been included. Finally, for statistical reasons investigators have usually had to be content with employing one rate of interest as an indicator instead of including the yields on a variety of financial assets simultaneously. With these simplifications the demand function can be written as:

$$M = f(P, r, Y_p, u),$$

with W substituted for Y_p in some instances.

1. If Y_p is an estimate of total annual income and r is 'the' rate of interest, Y_p/r, which is the capital value of a perpetual income stream Y_p, is a measure of total wealth. With r constant, changes in Y_p would be proportional to changes in wealth.

As this demand function stands there would be nothing to prevent a proportionate increase in prices and in the money value of all assets resulting in a non-proportionate increase in the demand for money holdings. This is thought to be implausible, since it is surely likely that the demand for money will be a demand for *real* balances, i.e. it will be independent of the scale which is used to measure values. Accordingly the demand function for real balances is obtained by dividing throughout by P:

$$\frac{M}{P} = f\left(r, \frac{Y_p}{P}, u\right) \quad \text{or} \quad \frac{M}{P} = f\left(r, \frac{W}{P}, u\right).$$

The main differences between the demand functions derived from the modern quantity theory and the Keynesian approach are the quantity theory's inclusion of wealth as opposed to current income, and the omission of any unstable element, such as is implied by the speculative demand for money. The latter is not ruled out in theory – interest-rate expectations appear in a full specification of the demand function – but it has not been included in practice. There are also two differences of emphasis. The quantity theory gives much more weight to prices – both in its long-standing concern with the proportionality between money and prices and more recently with expected inflation as an influence on the cost of holding money. In contrast, the interest rate on bonds is not given special prominence by the quantity theorists, who do not generally expect to find that the interest-elasticity of demand for money is high; whereas Keynesian theorists readily envisage circumstances in which the demand for money could be highly elastic with respect to interest rates.

5 The Demand for Money: Evidence

Before any theory can be tested it is necessary to settle on empirical measures of the theoretical concepts. When it comes to testing theories of the demand for money this is by no means an easy matter. The main difficulties arise in finding or selecting suitable measures of wealth or income, of rates of interest, and of money itself. Econometric studies of the demand for money have now been carried out in many countries, and the literature is much too extensive to be reviewed comprehensively here. Instead we shall concentrate on the results obtained in studies of the USA and UK and on studies which pay special attention to the influence of price inflation.

The distinctive feature of money – its use as a medium of exchange – suggests that any measure of money must include currency and deposits with commercial banks which can be withdrawn on demand (demand deposits in the USA and current accounts in the UK). This much is not in dispute. However, the question arises of whether a broader definition of money should be employed, including other deposit liabilities of the commercial banks which, at least in principle, can be withdrawn only after a period of notice has elapsed.

Some investigators have gone further and included the liabilities of other deposit-taking institutions, such as savings and loan associations in the USA and savings banks in Britain, in their definition of money on the grounds that their fixed monetary value and ease of encashment make them extremely good substitutes for interest-bearing bank deposits.

Within the group of assets which by virtue of their economic functions might reasonably be included in a measure of money there are two criteria for choosing between alternatives. Firstly, if a stable demand relationship can be established using one measure but not using another the former should be employed – in the absence of a stable relationship the theory cannot explain or predict economic behaviour. Secondly, if more than one measure satisfies this criterion the relevance of the measure for economic policy should be considered. If policy measures can be confined to currency and bank deposits, without bringing in complications from other financial intermediaries, so much the better; if policy cannot distinguish between current and deposit accounts a theory which focused on one but omitted the other would be of little value. In our discussion of the empirical evidence we shall consider studies using either a narrow definition or including time deposits but shall not deal with studies which have taken even broader aggregates of assets.

For the United States (non-human) wealth statistics over a considerable time span are available, but as yet no satisfactory wealth statistics over an extended period have been compiled for the UK. In the latter, studies have been restricted to the use of Y_p and Y. In both countries Y_p has been constructed from the series of current income, taking an average of incomes over a period of years and giving greater weight to the more recent observations. Since total wealth, including human wealth, can be estimated as the discounted value of the permanent income stream, Y_p can be treated as a proxy for wealth. Empirical studies based upon the modern quantity theory approach have usually included Y_p or W, but not both, as explanatory variables since total wealth for which Y_p is a proxy includes non-human wealth, W. Studies based upon a transactions approach or Keynesian theory emphasize Y. In the United States some investigators have tested all three possibilities.

The choice of interest rate is dictated partly by the availability of suitable statistics and partly by the investigator's theoretical approach. The Keynesian might naturally employ a long-term rate of interest, such as the yield on twenty-year bonds in the USA or the yield on consols in the UK, because this is central to liquidity preference theory. However, in the light of the theoretical work on the relation between the transactions demand and interest rates he would also be entitled to choose a short rate of interest on, for example, commercial bills in the USA or treasury bills in

Britain. For narrowly defined money the rate of interest offered on time deposits with the commercial banks may also be important. The quantity theorist might select a long-term rate, following Friedman's theoretical approach, or a short-term rate because the key interest rates in explaining the demand for money are likely to be those of the closest substitutes. Since theory gives no clear-cut answer on the choice of interest rates, empirical studies usually try out a variety of interest rates and see which contributes most to the explanation of the demand for money. When price expectations are included as a cost of holding money some proxy measure for the expected rate of inflation must also be found.

In most studies of the demand for money a logarithmic relationship has been specified, making use of some variant of the following basic form:

$$\ln \frac{M}{P} = a + b \ln \frac{Y}{P} + c \ln r.$$

With this form both the income-elasticity and interest-elasticity of demand for real balances are constant, and are measured by the coefficients b and c respectively. Of course Y_p may be substituted for Y and several interest rates may be included in the equation.

It is appropriate to link the current level of real balances to the current levels of income and interest rates only if desired money holdings are determined by reference to the current values of these other factors and if actual holdings can be adjusted to desired holdings within the data period. An alternative formulation has usually been specified in studies employing quarterly data; this allows for the possibility that money balances may be adjusted to their desired levels gradually or that the desired level may itself reflect experience of Y and r over a more extended period. Thus:

$$\ln \frac{M}{P} = a + b \ln \frac{Y}{P} + c \ln r + d \ln \left(\frac{M}{P}\right) - 1$$

where $\left(\frac{M}{P}\right) - 1$ is the level of real balances in the previous period. In this equation $(1 - d)$ is a measure of the speed of adjustment, and the income and interest-elasticities of the equilibrium demand for real balances are measured by $b/(1 - d)$ and $c/(1 - d)$ respectively.[1]

Before turning to examine empirical evidence we must be aware of one further statistical problem. Simply specifying a relationship between the quantity of money and a number of explanatory variables does not guarantee that the parameters estimated will reflect a *demand* relationship: in theory it could just as well be a supply relationship or some combination of supply and demand.

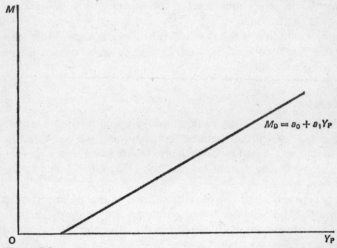

Figure 5.1

Consider, for example, the relationship between M and Y_p. Figure 5.1 shows a linear demand relationship. The quantity of money demanded, M_D, rises with permanent income Y_p. Now as permanent income rises in the long run, financial institutions generally are likely to expand, so that M_S, the quantity

1. The hypothesis that adjustment to the desired level is gradual is known as the *partial adjustment* hypothesis, and the hypothesis that the desired level depends on more extended experience is the *adaptive expectations* hypothesis. The equation cited reflects a very simple process of adjustment or adaptation, and other processes or the coexistence of partial adjustment and adaptive expectations lead to a more complex equation form.

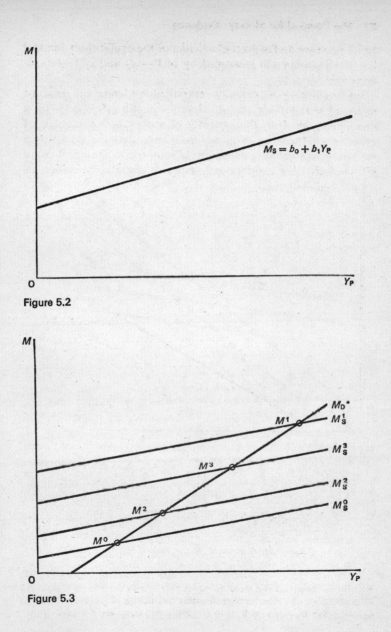

$M_S = b_0 + b_1 Y_P$

Figure 5.2

M_D

M_S^1

M^1

M_S^3

M^3

M_S^2

M^2

M_S^0

M^0

Figure 5.3

of money supplied, may also rise with Y_p as is shown in Figure 5.2. If we assume that any observation represents an equilibrium, each observation must lie on the intersection of some supply and some demand curve, such as M^0 in Figure 5.3. If the supply curve shifts while the demand curve remains stable we shall obtain a series of points, $M^0, M^1, M^2, M^3, \ldots$ which traces out the demand curve, e.g. Figure 5.3; but equally if the demand curve shifted

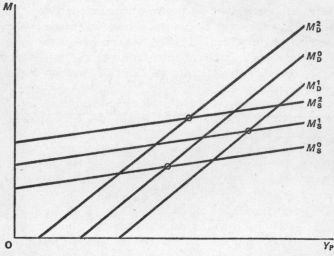

Figure 5.4

while the supply curve remained stable the points would trace out the supply curve and if both curves shift neither curve is identified; see Figure 5.4. Single equation methods are not sufficient to identify as a demand curve the relationship we estimate.

Fortunately there are two reasons for believing that most investigations have in fact uncovered demand rather than supply functions. Firstly, simultaneous equation methods employed in studying data for the USA tend to confirm the parameter estimates obtained by single equation methods. Secondly, consideration of the factors which determine the supply of money, particularly in the USA, suggest that M_S is likely to vary inde-

pendently of changes in the demand function at least in the short
run. This means that if the demand function is stable we should
be able to observe it; and if it is unstable we are unlikely to find
any clear relationship at all.

Empirical evidence: USA

Econometric studies of the demand for money in the USA have
typically employed either annual data over a long run of years or
quarterly data for part of the postwar period since 1945. The
results of the longer-term studies have been well surveyed by
Laidler (1969), while Goldfeld (1973) has carried out the most
recent comprehensive study of short-term postwar behaviour.
His work uses quarterly data from 1952 to 1972, and supersedes
earlier studies of this kind.

Long-run studies suggested that stable demand functions could
be found for both narrowly-defined money, M_1, consisting of
currency and demand deposits, and the broader measure, M_2,
which also includes time-deposits. There was little to choose
between the two measures. In contrast, Goldfeld's work shows
that the narrow measure is definitely preferable. The equation for
M_1 gave a good fit and there was no evidence of instability,
whereas the performance of M_2 was poorer and there was
evidence of structural shifts. In fact, Goldfeld found that dividing
M_1 into currency and demand deposits separately gave more
satisfactory results than treating M_1 as a whole.

On the choice between wealth or permanent income on the one
hand and current income on the other as determinants of the
demand for money there is again some conflict between the long-
run and short-run evidence. For example, Laidler (1966) found
that both W and Y_p explained long-run behaviour better than Y.
The superiority of wealth measures indicated that the asset
approach was preferable to the transactions approach in explaining long-run demand. But postwar short-run experience tells a
different story. Goldfeld found that income was clearly superior
to wealth as an element in the demand function, and concluded
that the transactions approach made sense.[1] The estimates of the

1. Since permanent income is generated from income experience by
means of an adaptive expectations process there are statistical difficulties in

income-elasticity of demand for M_2 obtained from long-run data are generally just over 1, though it has been lower in the last thirty years, whereas Goldfeld's estimate of the comparable elasticity for M_1 is 0·68, i.e. the demand for narrow money holdings rises less than in proportion to real income.

The evidence on the interest-elasticity of the demand for money is remarkably consistent. With respect to r_l the elasticity of the demand for money M_1 in the long run was estimated as about −0·7. Alternatively if M_1 is related to r_s the elasticity is about −0·2; the lower value of the elasticity can be attributed to the greater range of variation in r_s compared with r_l. Although Goldfeld used different measures of short-term interest rates his results did not conflict with those obtained in long-run studies. These elasticities mean that a rise in the long-term rate of interest from, say, 5 per cent to 5½ per cent (a 10 per cent rise) would typically be associated with a fall in the demand for money of about 7 per cent; to achieve approximately the same effect the short-term rate of interest would need to rise from, say, 4½ per cent to 6 per cent (a 33 per cent rise). Since changes in interest rates of this order are by no means unusual within the period of a business cycle it can be seen that interest rates have had a considerable influence on the demand for money.

This evidence is sufficient to dispose of the most rigid version of the quantity theory – one cannot now argue convincingly as if money and output are linked by a fixed technical coefficient – but it does not discriminate between the Keynesian and the modern quantity theorist. There have consequently been several attempts to study the characteristics of the liquidity preference curve in more detail. First of all, is there any evidence of a liquidity trap? If a liquidity trap exists one would expect the elasticity of M_D with respect to r to be greater at low than at high interest rates. Bronfenbrenner and Mayer (1960) and Laidler (1966) have tested to see whether this was so in American experience, using both M_1 and M_2 measures of money and both short and long-term interest rates, but they found no evidence to support the liquidity trap hypothesis.

---

choosing between Y_p and Y if money holdings also reflect a partial adjustment or adaptive expectations process.

It might be objected, however, that it is not strictly the absolute level of the interest rate which is important in Keynesian theory, but the interest rate in relation to the 'safe' or normal level; and this may change. Starleaf and Reimer (1967) carried out a test to see whether taking the difference between the current rate of interest and a measure of the normal rate – a weighted average of past interest rates calculated in a way and over a period analogous to permanent income – helped to explain the demand for money. It did not. While the appropriateness of the measure they used for the normal rate of interest might be questioned, the best that one can say of this particular feature of liquidity preference theory is that no evidence to support it in the USA has yet been found.

All the theoretical models predict that the demand for money in nominal terms will be proportional to the price level – in other words the demand for money should be expressed as a demand for *real* rather than nominal balances. Tests have confirmed that this hypothesis is justified. The influence in practice of expected changes in prices is more questionable. In the long run the relatively modest rates of price inflation and deflation experienced in the USA do not seem to have had any perceptible influence on the demand for real balances, though Goldfeld's study does provide some tentative evidence of price expectations affecting demand; but this evidence is certainly not conclusive.

The studies employing quarterly data have generally shown that the demand for money does not adjust instantaneously to the level of income and interest rates. But adjustment is fairly rapid and the bulk takes place within a year.[1]

Finally attempts have been made to estimate the demand for money by each of the main sectors of the economy. The demand by households is explained quite well by conventional theory, and that of financial institutions also fits into the standard framework. But neither the demand by business nor by state and local governments could be explained at all well. This is perhaps not very

1. On the adaptive expectations hypothesis the rate of adaptation may vary between the different factors influencing the demand for money. Goldfeld's results suggest that the rate of adaptation to interest rate changes is slightly faster than to changes in income.

surprising, since most of the theory underlying the demand functions has been constructed with households in mind. Nevertheless, it is rather disturbing, because failure to explain the behaviour of major groups of money holders inevitably casts some doubt on the future stability of the aggregate relationships which have been observed.

Empirical evidence: UK

As in the USA, empirical studies of the demand for money in the UK over a long period have been carried out using annual data, while shorter-run studies in the last twenty years or so have employed quarterly data. The pioneering study of the demand for money from 1877 to 1961 was carried out by Kavanagh and Walters (1966), and work completed before 1970 was surveyed by Goodhart and Crockett (1970). The most recent published empirical study is by Hacche (1974). Both narrow and broad money concepts have been used. Older studies often concentrated on the London clearing banks, taking as money either currency and these banks' current account deposits (M_1) or currency and all deposits (M_2). More recently work has employed the official measures of money, namely M_1 and M_3 as defined on pages 17 and 18.

Kavanagh and Walters showed that over a long run of years the demand for money was reasonably predictable in terms of income and interest rate variables, though they found that behaviour from 1945 to 1961 was less easy to explain. In his recent study Hacche also found it possible to obtain satisfactory explanations for both M_1 and M_3 over the period from the fourth quarter of 1963 until the third quarter of 1971, when the monetary control arrangements in the UK were changed. But the equations he fitted did not predict behaviour well in the next year and a half – particularly the equation for M_3. This seems to imply that the demand for money is rather sensitive to the prevailing institutional arrangements, and when structural changes alter the relative competitive strengths of banks and other financial institutions the demand for bank deposits is affected. Substitution is, of course, likely to be stronger between interest-bearing time deposits with banks and with other institutions than between current accounts (and currency) and time deposits generally. What this means is that relationships which seem to be reasonably well established under one institutional framework cannot be relied upon if the institutional structure changes.

Most estimates of the income-elasticity of the demand for money in the UK have been considerably below unity. Hacche found elasticities of under 0·5 for both M_1 and M_3 for the period 1963(4) to 1971(3), though these rose to 0·7 and 1·0 respectively when the data period was extended to 1971–(4). Statistically significant interest-elasticities have also been found, though again values vary with the specification of the equation and the time-period covered. For example, Hacche estimated the elasticity of M_1 with respect to the short-term rate of interest as between −0·05 and −0·10 and with respect to the long-term rate as about −0·2. For M_3 short-term rates of interest seem to be much more important than long-term, suggesting perhaps that broadly defined money should be seen primarily as a substitute for other liquid financial assets with a fixed capital value.

While there is no evidence against the view that money holdings are proportional to prices in the long run Hacche allows for a gradual process of adjustment in the short run. Thus an increase in nominal income due to inflation was not associated immediately with a proportional increase in money holdings, and the rate of adjustment was estimated as between 45 per cent and 60 per cent a quarter for M_1 and between 20 per cent and 35 per cent for M_3, depending on the period covered in the statistical analysis. No effects of expected price inflation on the demand for money have been observed yet in the UK, but studies have not taken account of the more rapid rate of inflation encountered in the mid 1970s. Some work on the demand for money by individual sectors of the economy has been carried out; as in the USA, attempts to explain the behaviour of households have been much more successful than those of companies.

To sum up, although less work has been done in the UK than in the USA the results obtained seem to be broadly consistent. In the absence of usable wealth statistics a comparison of wealth and income as determinants of money holdings is not possible in the UK, but in both countries the income-elasticity of demand for M_1 seems to be less than unity and interest rates have a significant effect. However, in recent years the demand for money does seem to have been less stable in the UK than in the USA.

Inflation and the demand for money

Rising prices impose costs on money holders, since the purchasing power of their money balances falls. And, while the expectation of rising prices generally raises interest rates, the return on bank deposits usually rises less rapidly and currency does not bear interest. Changes in the anticipated rate of inflation are reflected therefore in changes in the opportunity cost of holding money. This is an important element in the monetarists' model of the demand for money, according to which an increase in the expected rate of price inflation will reduce the demand for money. In hyper-inflationary conditions – when prices rise by some 50 per cent per month or more – Cagan (1956) and Allais (1966) have confirmed this prediction. Cagan analysed seven European hyper-inflations which occurred in the early 1920s and at the end of the Second World War, and showed that a measure of the expected rate of change of prices accounted for most of the changes in real cash balances held. Moreover, greater expected rates of inflation were associated with higher elasticities of demand for money with respect to the rate of inflation; price increases were shown to have an increasing effect on the demand for money. Allais's more recent study gives an improved explanation of some parts of hyper-inflationary conditions and has been applied to normal conditions in France, the UK and the USA.

Campbell (1970), Deaver (1970) and Diz (1970) have also shown that variations in the expected rate of inflation influenced equilibrium money balances in Brazil and Korea, Chile and Argentina respectively. Inflation was rapid in all these countries, though conditions fell far short of hyper-inflation. Finally, in a cross-section study of countries during 1959–63, Wallich (1967) also found that differences in the rate of inflation had a small but significant effect on the demand for money.

In all the single country studies expected inflation was assumed to reflect past experience, and the rate at which people adjust their expectations seems to increase with the rate at which prices are increasing. This may account for the failure of most empirical studies to detect any effect of price changes on equilibrium real balances in countries where prices have been reasonably stable. But when inflation is faster and more variable, people become much more aware of the cost of holding money and do appear to adjust their holdings as their estimate of that cost varies.

Empirical evidence: conclusion

The factors which theorists claimed would influence the demand for money have been shown to be important in practice. In the long run the most important influences are probably income and prices – money holdings rise with real income and/or wealth, and equilibrium holdings are proportional to prices. But money is also substituted for other financial assets and goods – holdings vary systematically with interest rates and the anticipated rate of inflation. Which interest rates are most relevant seems to reflect the breadth of the concept of money employed and the prevailing institutional conditions.

No compelling evidence for the existence of a liquidity trap has been found, but the short-run stability of the demand for money is still questionable. In particular, UK (and Canadian) experience shows that major changes in the institutional framework governing financial institutions are likely to be associated with shifts in the demand function. Apart from such shifts, reasonably stable and well-defined demand functions do seem to exist in the long run.

The demand for money by individual sectors of the economy is one area in which further work is needed. The conventional kind of model seems to apply satisfactorily to the household sector, but for other sectors it is less successful. Until the behaviour of these sectors is also understood some doubt about the stability of the observed relationships for the aggregate demand for money must remain.

6 Money, Economic Activity and Prices

Introduction

Just as we found that there are a number of alternative theoretical approaches to analysing the demand for money, so we find contrasting views of the mechanism through which monetary controls may be expected to influence the economy. On the one hand some theorists put the emphasis on a direct relation between the money supply and expenditure – reversing the demand relationship already discussed under the rigid quantity theory of money – and on the other hand there are some who argue that it is by changing financial conditions, particularly rates of interest, and so influencing the volumes of lending and borrowing, that monetary controls impinge upon the economy.

According to the former school of thought an increase in the supply of money means that some money holders will have excess money balances in their asset portfolios. In the process of restoring equilibrium these balances will be converted into real goods and services either directly or through the intermediation of financial institutions. The pressure of demand for goods and services will stimulate output and encourage price rises until the value of output has risen in proportion to the increase in the money supply. This monetarist school gives no special emphasis to the rates of interest on the more common financial assets. They are also usually more concerned about the long-run link between money and prices than with the effects of monetary conditions on output, since in the long run output is determined by the resources available to an economy and their productivity in use.

The latter school sees the main direct impact of a change in the money supply on observable rates of interest, and emphasizes the effect of a change in the money supply on the cost and availability of credit. A fall in the rate charged to borrowers may stimulate consumption and investment directly, or a general easing in financial conditions following a rise in the money supply may encourage financial institutions to make funds more readily available to potential borrowers, thus allowing borrowers to tap relatively low-cost sources of funds and making funds available to some borrowers who might otherwise have been unable to obtain them on any tolerable terms. The analytical framework employed by this school is generally Keynesian in character, and their primary concern is the effect of monetary policy on economic activity, rather than on prices.

Money multipliers

Those economists who hold that there is a direct link from the money supply to the level of income, rather than an indirect connection through interest rates, do not deny that indirect effects may exist. They argue only that measured interest rates are poor indicators of the wide range of implicit rates of interest which are likely to be relevant, and that in any case the effect of changes in measured interest rates on consumption or investment will be included in a direct statistical analysis. When the money supply increases people find that their money balances have risen above their normal requirements. To run them down they are just as likely to buy goods and services as to buy financial assets. While purchases of financial assets may affect measured rates of interest immediately, they may also influence credit conditions other than interest rates: for example, if non-bank financial institutions, such as building societies in Britain or savings and loan associations in the USA, receive more deposits they are likely at first to lend to more borrowers and to advance up to a larger proportion of the value of property rather than reduce the rate of interest to borrowers. Those borrowers who find they can obtain more funds are likely to spend a larger amount on new furnishings and equipment for their property, and so expenditure rises without there being any change in measured interest rates. Moreover, the borrowed money which is spent by some becomes income and higher cash balances for others, and they too react by spending more. The monetarist school argues that such reactions will continue until nominal income flows have been brought back into balance with the increased stock of money, so that people generally are content to hold the money which has been created. Theories which concentrate on effects which can be traced directly to movements in measured interest rates are misleading because they do not take account explicitly of these other important effects on expenditure.

It is no part of this line of argument, however, that the change in expenditure will follow *immediately* after a change in the money supply. In the short run people may hold extra balances or tolerate lower balances for a while, and at some cost or inconvenience to spenders the credit mechanism may prevent a reduction in the money supply from being immediately reflected in lower expenditure. But this, it is argued, is a transient phenomenon. While there is some elasticity in the system, pressures for a return to the norm are set up as soon as the system is distorted. Thus a change in the money supply will be reflected *eventually* in a proportional change in the value of income. There is considerable uncertainty surrounding the time needed for adjustment, although it seems likely that there will be a significant effect on expenditure within six months: the total adjustment is unlikely to extend over more than two years.

The *money multiplier* summarizes the relation between money and income: it measures the equilibrium change in income caused by a unit change in the supply of money. The concept is analogous to that of the familiar Keynesian multiplier in the theory of income determination: taking the simplest Keynesian model, if the level of investment can be treated as autonomous and if a stable relationship (the consumption function) exists linking consumption with income, then the income multiplier measures the total change in income which is induced by a unit change in investment. Likewise, if the supply of money can be treated as autonomous and if a stable relationship (the demand for money) exists linking money and income, then the money multiplier measures the change in equilibrium income caused by a unit change in the money supply.

The two 'ifs' in this statement must be emphasized. A causal relationship from money to income can exist only if the money supply is determined independently of the level of income. The extent to which this has been true in different countries at various times is a subject of much debate. Some economists have argued that during certain periods in the UK and the USA the money supply could for practical purposes be treated as exogenous, but at other times it seems likely that there was a strong feedback from income to money; indeed the direction of causation may have been reversed.

The nature and stability of the demand for money was discussed at length in the previous chapter. Studies of the money multiplier have been based on the hypothesis that the demand for money is a function of permanent income, so that it is related to past as well as present income levels, and no explicit account has been taken of the rate of interest. As we have already noted this can be justified by the argument that indirect effects due to changes in interest rates will be picked up in the statistical analysis; further, in accordance with classical economic thought, it is asserted that a change in the money supply can have only a temporary effect on the real rate of interest, which is determined in the long run by real rather than monetary factors (see Friedman, 1968).

Empirical investigation of the causal role of money has taken two forms. First of all, *timing* evidence has been adduced in support of this view. In the USA Friedman (1961) compared the timing of peaks and troughs in the *rate of change* of the money supply with the peaks and troughs in the *level* of economic activity. He found that on average economic activity lagged behind the money supply by an average of sixteen months for the peaks and twelve months for the troughs, but there was a considerable dispersion about these average figures. Goodhart and Crockett (1970) report that the lag pattern in the relationship between money and income in the UK is complex; correlations between changes in the money stock and subsequent changes in income had two peaks, one when money led income by only two or three months and the other when money had a much longer lead of over a year. However, this kind of evidence is far from conclusive, because there are many reasons why people might wish to build up money balances in advance of expenditure, and unless the money stock is determined quite independently of the demand for money the observed association might merely reflect the influence of some common causes rather than a causal sequence running from money to income.

A second kind of investigation has employed regression analysis to study the relationship between the change in the nominal value of some measure of national product and the concurrent and preceding changes in the money stock. Friedman and Schwartz (1963b) found a stable long-run relationship, and more recent work in the USA, e.g. Andersen and Jordan (1968) has also shown a strong connection.

In the UK Walters (1966) carried out a similar kind of investigation of the relationship at different times over a period of some eighty years. In the three decades prior to 1914 he argues that the supply of money can be treated as autonomous: Bank rate was the principal weapon of monetary policy, and in his opinion changes in Bank rate were determined mainly by gold movements which had only a tenuous link with domestic economic conditions. His results for this period suggest that a 1 per cent increase in the supply of money, if it really was autonomous, caused rather less than a 1 per cent increase in gross national product, with about half the effect observed in the current and half in the following year. An analysis of data for 1922 to 1938 appears at first sight to confirm these results, but, as Walters himself argues, it is difficult to believe that the money supply was autonomous for much of this period: from 1932 onwards it seems much more likely that the money supply responded to changes in the demand while the authorities pursued a cheap money policy. A study of quarterly data from late 1955 to 1962 gave nonsense results: the government's attempts to achieve stability of prices and income in this period ensured that the supply of money was by no means autonomous, and the money multiplier was not important. More recent studies, e.g. Artis and Nobay (1969), have confirmed this result.

The money supply controversy

This approach has also been used to compare the response of income to changes in the money supply with its response to changes in 'autonomous expenditure' – comparing in effect the stability of the monetary multiplier with the stability of the Keynesian multiplier. Friedman and Meiselman (1963) set out to do this by comparing simple versions of the quantity theory and Keynesian theory over long periods. They concluded that, except for the 1930s, the money supply was more important than autonomous expenditure as a determinant of income. However, although much more work on similar lines has been done in the USA and elsewhere, their analysis and conclusions have not been accepted uncritically by economists in general. The methodology of this approach to the study of both Keynesian and money multipliers, and the particular measures they employed, have been subjected to severe attack.

The first methodological criticism is directed at the single equation approach which has been adopted. Critics argue that a simultaneous equation system is necessary to take account of the complex of interrelations and feedbacks in an economy. Single equations throw little light on the economic structure: as Edge (1967) demonstrates, only two of the six equations tested by Friedman and Meiselman can be derived from their simple structural models. Using a more complex model Ando and Modigliani (1965) showed that both money and autonomous expenditure affected income, the latter having the greater effect.

The other major methodological issue is the extent to which the money supply or 'autonomous expenditure' is truly autonomous. It seems unlikely that the money supply was exogenous in the 1930s, or in the war years when the monetary model apparently performs well and the Keynesian model very badly. And in the postwar period, when governments and the monetary authorities in both the USA and the UK have attempted to follow counter-cyclical policies, the levels of autonomous expenditure and the money stock have been adjusted in relation to the actual or anticipated levels of income. In these circumstances neither can be regarded as autonomous. Furthermore, in so far as counter-cyclical policy may have been successful, any relationship between money or autonomous expenditure and the level of income will be obscured, because the fluctuations which would otherwise have taken place in income will have been moderated. It is also noticeable that whereas in the USA the money multiplier has generally been found to be larger and more stable than the Keynesian multiplier in recent work, the reverse is true for the UK, where throughout the 1950s and 1960s the authorities generally tried to control interest rates and allowed the demand for money to determine the money stock.

In conclusion, the monetarist view of the link between money and economic activity seems most appropriate in countries or at times when the money stock has been determined without reference to the level of national income. Where monetary policy has been employed as one element in counter-cyclical economic policy this condition is not satisfied, and a view of the relationship which takes more account of the simultaneity between money and income in these circumstances is likely to be more fruitful.

The Keynesian approach

Writers in the Keynesian tradition give much more prominence to the effects of a change in the money stock on financial markets and the behaviour of financial institutions, in contrast to the monetarists' emphasis upon direct substitutability between money and goods. A contraction of the money stock brought about through open market sales of securities by the central bank has its immediate impact on the rate of interest on these securities, and as the capital market as a whole adjusts to the change in this particular interest rate there are further effects upon the cost of capital, the value of other securities and the terms on which credit is available from banks and other financial institutions. These changes in financial conditions influence spending on goods and services, and the initial impact is multiplied through the standard Keynesian multiplier process. The extent and timing of the effect of a change in the money stock on the level of expenditure therefore depends on the one hand on the reaction of interest rates and the response of financial institutions to the initial change in money and on the other hand on the effect of these changes in financial conditions on expenditures. We shall deal first with the effect associated with changing interest rates and leave a discussion of credit availability and the behaviour of financial institutions until later.

Empirical studies of the demand for money have shown that the desired stock of money is influenced by the level of the interest rate. This means that, other things being equal, a change in the stock of money will be associated with a change in interest rates, and since the evidence indicates that the interest-elasticity of demand is fairly low such a change in interest rates will be by no means insignificant. Only if the demand for money were infinitely elastic to interest rates (i.e. a liquidity trap situation existed) would there be no reaction to a change in the stock of money, and the empirical evidence seems to rule this out.

But will a change in interest rates affect the level of expenditure? While an investment demand schedule linking investment to the rate of interest is a key element in the Keynesian theoretical model, theorists in this tradition have often been sceptical about the interest-elasticity of this schedule. They have argued that in practice investment was likely to be rather insensitive to changes in the rate of interest. However, more recent theoretical discussion has shown that changes in the rate of interest are likely to have quite substantial effects upon investment in long-lived durable goods, and the view that the interest-elasticity would be significant has been confirmed in empirical studies. Thus monetary policy can reasonably be expected to affect economic activity through an interest-rate channel.

Changes in interest rates also have a wealth effect – when interest rates fall the capital values of long-term debt instruments rise, the values of equity shares usually rise too and so do the prices of existing physical assets such as housing. Thus wealth owners feel better off – the capital value of their wealth has risen in relation to income – and this is reflected in higher consumption spending. The higher value of existing wealth makes new saving less necessary, and people feel tempted to take advantage of capital gains in the form of increased consumption. Thus a second channel through which monetary policy affects expenditure is a wealth effect on consumption.

A third channel depends upon the behaviour of financial institutions. Banks and other deposit-taking institutions which make loans to private borrowers generally set a standard rate of interest on these loans and vary other conditions according to the funds they have available. For example, when banks are short of funds they insist on better security for loans than when they wish to expand their lending business. Building societies in the UK and savings and loan associations in the USA require potential borrowers to provide a larger percentage of the price of a house when funds are tight than when they are easy, and may also impose a lower limit on the amount borrowed in relation to the borrower's income. In the short run the reaction to a change in the inflow of funds to such financial institutions usually takes the form of varying these non-price aspects of loan business, and only if the variation in inflow is expected to persist will the financial institutions also change their price. In consequence, variations in the availability of credit can take place independently of the rates of interest charged for loans. While an inability to obtain funds from the most convenient or cheapest source may not always deter a potential borrower altogether, it often means that he is forced to find an alternative source of finance at a considerably higher rate of interest, and this jump in the cost of funds – which can be distinguished from a change in the general level of interest rates – is likely to have a substantial deterrent effect. Changes in the availability of credit to some borrowers may also take place independently of changes in the stock of money in countries where the monetary authorities regulate the lending activities of the banks and other financial institutions.

Credit rationing is a sign of disequilibrium within the financial system. If the rate of interest charged on bank loans is too low in relation to the cost of deposits or interest earned on other assets, then for a time banks may tend to restrict their lending in other ways. But ultimately, unless the authorities prohibit any change, they will raise the interest rate on bank loans and return the other terms of lending to normal. Credit rationing is thus a temporary phenomenon if financial institutions are permitted to compete freely. How much takes place depends very much on the institutional framework in each country. As noted below, studies in the United States have found that credit rationing plays an important role in the housing market, and the same is undoubtedly true of the UK.

Non-bank financial institutions

The influence of non-bank financial institutions, which compete with banks on both the borrowing and lending sides of their business, has been the subject of much controversy. They affect the relationship between money and economic activity in three ways: their existence alters the equilibrium relationship between money holdings and the level of income, they affect the interest-sensitivity of the demand for money, and their activities influence the time-response of economic activity to monetary impulses.

If the liabilities of non-bank financial institutions are good substitutes for money in some of its functions their existence reduces the demand for money. For example, in Britain savings banks and building societies compete with commercial banks for the deposits of the general public. Even if these deposits cannot be used as a medium of exchange, they perform the same store of value function as bank deposits and they also bear interest, frequently at a higher rate than that offered by the commercial banks. Instead of holding savings with the banks some people therefore choose to hold part or all of their savings with these other deposit-taking institutions. To the extent that they do so the demand for money is reduced. This means that the ratio of money to national income is also reduced and the size of the money multiplier is increased: if more money is created national income has to rise sufficiently to absorb the additional money into people's desired balances.

Secondly, the existence of non-bank financial institutions reduces but does not eliminate the impact of a change in the money stock upon the rate of interest. Suppose that the monetary authorities reduce the size of the reserve base available to the banks. This places the banks, who hold such reserves in their asset portfolios, at a competitive disadvantage relative to non-bank financial institutions which do not hold reserves in this form. Thus banks are less able to compete for deposits than formerly, or alternatively they must charge a higher rate of interest on loans to compensate for the increased cost of reserves. Non-bank financial institutions need not do this, and so are able to attract both deposits and lending business from the banks. But since bank deposits and the deposits of non-bank financial institutions are not perfect substitutes, and since in general non-banks engage in more specialized lending business, the extent to which they are able to substitute for banks is limited. Consequently the system cannot fully offset a contraction in the money stock through an expansion of non-bank institutions. Their effect then is to weaken the impact of monetary policy, but not to negate it altogether.[1]

Thirdly, through their effects upon the availability of credit, non-bank financial institutions influence the time-response of the economy to monetary action. If, when interest rates rise, mortgage-lending institutions are slow to respond and suffer a shortfall in the inflow of funds, credit rationing will ensue and activity in the housing market will be reduced. Moreover, if the banks are able to change their interest rates flexibly but lending practices prevent other specialized financial institutions from following suit, the effects of credit restriction or ease may be felt much more fully in the areas financed by these specialized institutions than in the remainder of the economy.

Empirical evidence: USA

Large-scale econometric models have usually incorporated a Keynesian approach to the linkage between money and economic activity in the structure. A good example is the FRB–MIT model reported by De Leeuw and Gramlich (1969). In their model action by the monetary authorities on the supply of high-powered money influences economic activity through all three channels. First of all it influences the cost of capital which impinges on

1. If monetary restrictions take the form of direct interference with the business of banks, but not of other financial institutions, the activities of these institutions are likely, eventually, to offset the restrictions on the banks almost completely. This is because the imposition of direct restrictions prevents the banks from competing with other financial institutions for business, with the result that the business which would have been done by the banks is gradually diverted to these other channels. The flow of credit is like a stream with many channels. When a major channel (such as the banks) is blocked water builds up initially behind the dam, and for a while the flow is reduced. But eventually the flow through the other channels increases and the dam is by-passed, until the total flow returns to its initial level.

producers' investment, residential construction, consumption, and expenditure by state and local governments. The responses are naturally rather complex functions of the cost of capital. For example, in the case of producers' investment the cost of capital influences the minimum rate of return which business must expect to earn on new investment, and this in turn helps to determine an optimum capital stock. If this is greater than the actual stock, orders for new capital goods are placed. Finally, the current level of investment is determined by the orders which were placed in the past. It follows that the response of investment to a change in the cost of capital is both delayed and distributed over an extended period. In broad terms the mechanism through which the rate of interest influences residential construction and expenditure by state and local government is similar, though the details differ. For consumption, the rate of interest influences the cost of credit and through this the sales of durable goods.

The second channel is the wealth effect on consumption. Consumer expenditure depends not only on income but also upon the net worth of households, including the market value of equity shares. The model includes a relationship between the yield on equity shares, and thus their price, and other interest rates which are affected more directly by monetary policy. Credit rationing affects the housing market through the supply of mortgage finance.

The third channel, credit rationing, is confined to the housing market. A restrictive monetary policy raises interest rates generally, but because their mortgage loans are usually at fixed rates of interest savings and loan associations find it difficult to raise the rates of interest paid to depositors correspondingly. The net inflow of deposits falls away, and the associations resort to credit rationing in allocating the limited funds available. Subsequently, when funds are again available more readily, there is a backlog of demand to make good.

De Leeuw and Gramlich use the model to ascertain the probable effects of a $1 billion increase in high-powered money. Table 6.1 shows the results over the first sixteen quarters. About half of the ultimate impact occurs within the first year, and eventually the total effect is about seven times the initial increase in high

Table 6.1 The Channels of Monetary Policy

Quarter	Total effect ($ billion)	Channel (%)		
		Cost of capital	Wealth	Credit rationing
4	3·5	49	34	17
8	5·4	48	43	9
12	6·8	51	44	5
16	7·0	66	45	−11

Source: De Leeuw and Gramlich (1969).

powered money. The cost of capital channel accounts for some two thirds of the total at the end of four years, but earlier the importance of this channel is rather less. The wealth effect accounts initially for about a third, rising later to nearly half of the total. Credit rationing is quite important initially, but subsequently reverses in significance as savings and loan associations gradually take action to return their asset portfolios towards an optimum position. The slow rise in the importance of the cost of capital channel reflects the very long response lag to this stimulus, whereas in contrast, the wealth effect on consumption builds up quite quickly, and indeed is much more important for consumption than the cost of capital.

Empirical evidence: UK

The Radcliffe Committee (1959), which reported on the working of the monetary system in the UK, were sceptical of the ability of monetary policy to influence spending. Their broad conclusion on the effect of monetary measures in the 1950s was that 'the monetary instruments employed left untouched the large industrial corporations which control more than half the investment in manufacturing industry and neither their planning nor that of the public corporations appears to have responded seriously to changes in interest rates. In the more fractionally organized parts of the private sector there has been pressure here and pressure there but nothing of great moment' (para. 472). This conclusion reflected the Committee's lack of success in finding evidence of any significant reaction to monetary restraint, which they attributed to the very high liquidity of companies in the early postwar years, and although there was a substantial running down of liquidity in 1955–7 the Committee were uncertain whether 'any important proportion of companies had by 1957 reached the point of being uncomfortably illiquid' (para. 479). So far as matters relevant to monetary policy were concerned the Committee assumed that the 1960s would resemble the 1950s, although they expressed doubt as to whether 'the private sector generally, and especially the parts most rapidly growing, could continue to be comparatively independent of financial conditions' (para. 486).

Subsequent experience demonstrated that their doubts were justified. Table 6.2 shows that although holdings of liquid assets rose by a third by 1970, bank advances rose by a factor of over six; and, from being net lenders to the banks, companies became net borrowers. Both liquid assets and bank advances have continued to grow rapidly since then, partly as a consequence of inflation. In particular, net liquidity fell precipitously in 1973 and 1974, since when there has been comparatively little change. The altered liquidity position from the early 1960s meant that companies were much more responsive to financial conditions than during the period immediately preceding the Radcliffe Committee's deliberations. In the last five years liquidity has been

Table 6.2 Liquidity of UK Industrial and Commercial
Companies, 1955–78

	Liquid assets (£ million)	Bank advances (£ million)	Net liquidity (£ million)
1955	3,247	969	2,278
1960	3,890	1,929	1,961
1965	3,890	3,785	105
1970	4,463	5,906	−1,443
1975	11,327	18,410	−7,083
1976	13,128	21,707	−8,579
1977	15,376	23,333	−7,957
1978	17,304	25,735	−8,431

Sources: *Financial Statistics*, April 1979, Table 9.3 and *Bank of England* (1970).

distinctly tight, and companies have taken steps to strengthen their balance sheets.

Companies have also had greater recourse to the capital market. As Table 6.3 shows, capital issues by industrial and commercial

Table 6.3 Capital Issues by UK Industrial and Commercial Companies

	Capital issues (£ million, annual average)
1953–57	196
1958–62	301
1963–67	429
1968–72	421
1973–77	514
1978	725

Sources: *Financial Statistics*, April 1979, Table 12.1 and *Bank of England* (1970).

companies averaged under £200 million per annum in the five years 1953–7, but they rose to an average of £300 million in the following five years, and to over £400 million in the next ten. Thanks to historically very high interest rates on long-term debentures and a collapse of equity prices, issues fell off dramatically in 1973 and 1974, but following a recovery in equity prices new capital issues reached record levels in 1975, as companies sought to fund part of the short-term debt incurred in the previous two years. Since then equity issues have remained substantial, though owing to the high level of interest rates very few issues of long-term debt have been made. Companies have continued to rely on the banks for short- and medium-term loans.

While it is not yet possible to quote systematic econometric studies which demonstrate that a shortage of credit has influenced fixed investment or stock-building, the statements of industrialists and informed observers of the industrial situation leave no doubt that this has in fact been so. To ease companies' immediate liquidity situation, and perhaps to strengthen their capital base so that potential lenders would be prepared to accept the risk of further lending, the government took measures at the end of 1974 which cut company tax payments due in early 1975 very substantially and thereby avoided a further strain on company liquidity.

The Radcliffe Committee also considered that changes in the rate of interest were unlikely to have much influence on industrial investment. It is worthwhile recalling their *a priori* reasoning (which was, of course, supported by the evidence submitted by industrialists). The rate of interest on borrowed funds was low in relation to the return expected from typical industrial investment projects, leaving a margin which would still be substantial even if interest rates rose: the real burden of interest (and capital) repayments was reduced by inflation, which was expected to continue; and since interest could be treated as a cost in computing taxable profits, the effect of any change in interest rates was mitigated by tax. How telling are these arguments in present conditions?

A preliminary point to notice is that in considering the influence of the cost of funds on investment it is not sufficient to concentrate on long-term bond yield. It is the cost of capital as a whole to the firm which is relevant for investment decisions and this is a weighted average of the cost of equity capital, of long-term fixed-interest borrowing, and of short-term borrowing.

Since the end of the 1950s there has been a narrowing of the gap between the cost of funds and the average rate of return on industrial investment. There has been a sharp rise in nominal rates of interest on short- and long-term debt, and while the anticipated rate of inflation has also risen, industrialists have been very unwilling to issue long-term debt at the rates of interest prevailing in recent years.[1] If the rate of inflation fell in the future the servicing of such debt would be very burdensome. While dividend yields have generally been lower than in the 1950s, these do not give an accurate guide to changes in the cost of equity capital, which must also make allowances for expected future increases in dividends. Moreover, the average rate of return on industrial investment has declined. Thus an increase in the cost of

1. The redemption yield on twenty-year loan stocks rose to nearly 20 per cent at the end of 1974.

funds may now make greater inroads into industrialists' profit margins, and while it is still true that tax does partially offset the increased cost of debt capital, this does not apply to equity.

Although econometric studies covering the very high nominal rates of interest in recent years have not yet been carried out, the results of some econometric studies of earlier years do seem to confirm that high interest rates deter company investment. For example, Hines and Catephores (1970) found an interest-elasticity of investment demand which lay well above unity, with an average lag of at least six or seven quarters, and Trivedi (1970) detected some interest-elasticity in inventory investment.

While consumer borrowing is undoubtedly important in determining consumption expenditure, it is not yet clear that borrowing in Britain responds to changes in interest rates. What is certain is that controls on instalment lending – through specifying a minimum deposit and maximum period for repayment – and requests to the banks to curtail their lending to persons have been reflected in new borrowing and particularly in purchases of consumer durable goods. The second channel of monetary policy – the wealth effect – also seems to influence consumer spending.[1] Studies of the personal sector's behaviour in the capital market also show that, while the personal sector is a steady net seller of company securities, the amount of funds realized is much greater when prices are high than when they are low. This is consistent with the notion that people tend to take capital gains when the opportunity arises, and that part of the funds realized will augment spending on goods and services.

In so far as banks ration credit to consumers, in deference to requests from the Bank of England, the credit rationing channel of monetary policy is also evident in Britain. But, just as in America the behaviour of savings and loan associations accounts for much of the impact through this channel, building societies in Britain, which are the dominant force in the provision of finance for private house-ownership, are probably the most important source of the credit-rationing effect.

In contrast with the USA, spending by British local government units is probably relatively insensitive to credit-market

1. See Hilton and Crossfield (1970).

conditions. This reflects the greater degree of centralized control over expenditure in the UK. Nevertheless, taken as a whole the evidence suggests that monetary policy influences expenditure in Britain through much the same mechanism as in the USA, though the strength of the effects in the various sectors and the time-lags involved must inevitably be affected by differences in institutional structure.

Money and prices

Whether one adopts a monetarist or a Keynesian approach one is led to the conclusion that a sharp or persistent increase in the stock of money will be associated with a broadly proportionate increase in prices. To be sure, if there is unemployment of labour and capital in the economy some moderate increase in the nominal stock of money may stimulate an increase in output rather than prices, but once a state of full employment has been reached any further monetary expansion will be inflationary.[1] Moreover, non-inflationary monetary expansion can take place only if there is a background of unemployment of *both* labour *and* capital in the economy, since if there is structural unemployment of labour, with capital fully employed at the going real wage rate, an expansion of aggregate demand which is not accompanied by a fall in real wages will raise the general price level without increasing the level of output. Thus theorists generally accept the proposition that a rapid increase in the money stock will lead to a rise in prices and that persistently rising prices cannot take place without associated monetary expansion.

There is, however, a very great divergence of view as to whether monetary expansion should be regarded as the prime cause of inflation. Many economists argue that it should, but there are others who see inflation as being caused primarily by other causes – frequently an effort by workers to increase their real incomes without any corresponding increase in productivity – and who regard the increase in money as merely accommodating this inflation. In their view the authorities are faced with a choice between, on the one hand, preserving price stability but allowing

1. As the economy approaches closer to full employment the proportion of the effect of monetary expansion on output falls and that on prices rises.

the attempts to increase real wages to cause unemployment in the economy and, on the other hand, of frustrating the efforts of organized labour by allowing price rises to offset the increases gained in money wages. The authorities choose to let the money stock expand because they regard inflation as the lesser of two evils. Against this, those who believe that money is the prime cause of inflation argue that this choice is open to the authorities only in the very short term and that organized labour will soon take note of the fact that its desire for higher real wages has been frustrated and demand ever larger increases in money wages, thus leading to an accelerating rate of inflation.

Suppose that labour unions are demanding and are successful in obtaining higher money wages. Within the private sector firms would normally react by pushing up the prices of their products, and in the public sector total wage bills would rise correspondingly. However, in the private sector the rise in prices and wages increases the demand for working capital and, unless the authorities allow bank loans to expand, firms will be forced to curtail their activities. Similarly, within the public sector if no additional finance is available employment must be cut back. Thus by controlling the money stock the authorities discourage expansion in the nominal value of aggregate demand and hence, with prices higher, reduce the volume of output and employment. But, at least in the short run, the authorities have the option of allowing monetary expansion to take place so that there is no cut back in real aggregate demand and output and employment are preserved. In that case, however, the labour unions will find that in spite of the increase in money wages the real wages of their members have not increased. The crucial question is: 'What happens next?' If, seeing that their real incomes have not increased, labour unions demand and obtain even larger increases in money wages then the authorities are faced again with the same situation and must tolerate either a rise in unemployment or an acceleration in the rate of inflation. If the labour unions are prepared to acquiesce in the real wages their members are earning the inflation can cease. Recent experience in the UK suggests that powerful labour unions are not prepared to see their gains in real income eroded by inflation so that attempts to prevent unemployment by monetary expansion are doomed to failure.

In these circumstances the real choice open to governments is the following. Either they curb the power of labour unions in order to prevent real wages rising to a level which creates unemployment or they allow that unemployment to arise. Since inflation cannot be allowed to *accelerate* indefinitely, monetary expansion as a cure is not a realistic option. If the government does allow the unemployment to arise it need not persist indefinitely, since that unemployment may itself weaken the monopolistic power of some unions, and to the extent that it does not do so competition will be increased in other parts of the labour market and real wages there will be reduced. The effect then will be to redistribute income from those whose bargaining power is weak to those whose power is stronger.

Since money wages are generally slow to change in a downward direction attempts to cure a rapid inflation by cutting back the rate of monetary expansion sharply would undoubtedly lead to heavy unemployment, unless linked to other measures which were effective in reducing the rates of increase of money wages and prices. The cure of inflation thus becomes a social and political question. It depends on the extent to which governments want and are able to intervene in labour markets to reduce the monopoly power of certain parts of organized labour; it depends on the extent to which society is prepared to tolerate unemployment; and it depends on the power of the government to gain acceptance for other measures which will allow it to influence the behaviour of wages and prices while reducing the rate of monetary expansion. To argue that monetary expansion is the sole cause of inflation is to ignore the social and political factors which cause governments to permit that monetary expansion to take place. But to believe that inflation can be cured without control of the money supply is to ignore what is probably the best documented and most researched relationship in economics – the relationship between the level of income and the demand for money.

7 Techniques of Monetary Control

General and specific control techniques

The instruments of monetary control considered in this chapter fall into two groups. On the one hand the authorities have at their disposal a set of instruments which affect certain key interest rates or which involve transactions in certain key markets; these instruments have a wide ranging impact on financial institutions generally and affect the cost and availability of capital funds and credit throughout the economy. On the other hand the authorities can employ a considerable number of specific instruments of control which apply to particular groups of financial institutions. Their primary impact is restricted to the institutions immediately concerned, although they also produce secondary repercussions in other institutions. These controls may be very effective when the financial system is dominated by the institutions concerned and when financial markets are not highly developed, but in sophisticated systems the secondary repercussions may go a long way towards negating the primary effect of the control.

An example illustrates this. Suppose the authorities placed a ceiling on the private-sector lending of just one bank, at a time when bank lending was expanding generally. The primary impact would be to deny funds to some customers of this particular bank, and in the very short run there might even be some reduction in their spending. But these customers would very soon approach other banks whose lending was uncontrolled, and obtain funds from them. (The controlled bank would compete less actively for deposits because it was not permitted to lend them profitably, and this would release the additional deposits required by the other banks to support their higher lending.) The end result would be a slight change in the channels through which credit flows, with no perceptible change in the availability or cost of credit in the economy as a whole.

This example seems rather absurd because no competent monetary authority would restrict just one bank while leaving the others completely uncontrolled. But the difference between this and some actual controls is one of degree rather than of kind. For example specific controls on major deposit banks in the U K were frustrated to the extent that new credit flows grew up which by-passed them. The larger the proportion of customary credit flows which are included in the controlled sector the more effective the controls will be because as the controls become more pervasive it becomes progressively less easy and more costly to by-pass them.

One should not underestimate the speed at which new financial institutions and markets can grow and substitute for the existing channels of finance in sophisticated financial systems, thus progressively weakening the initial impact of specific controls. To avoid this the authorities are likely to be compelled to spread the net of controls ever more widely, as experience in the U K has demonstrated. The effectiveness of specific controls depends in the short run on their ability to curb existing channels of finance; in the long run their effects, like those of general controls, reflect their impact on the cost and availability of finance from all sources to borrowers in the private sector.

General instruments of control

General instruments of control affect either the reserve base of the banking system or the interest rates prevailing in financial markets.[1] The most important technique is open-market operations in securities, and the implications of such operations for the money supply have already been discussed in Chapter 2. While purchases or sales of government securities which are not treated as reserves by the banks are the most common form of open-market operations in both the U K and the U S A, transactions in commercial bills may also be employed, and in some instances monetary authorities have also bought or sold foreign exchange (often on

1. Changes in interest rates and in the reserve base are, of course, interdependent.

terms which were favourable to the market) to try to insulate the reserve base from the effects of international capital flows.

When purchases or sales of government securities are the preferred instrument for open-market operations, the authorities frequently have a choice of the maturity of the debt in which they deal. Whether this choice affects the relative yields on long-dated as against short-dated securities is a question which has aroused much debate. It turns on the nature of the determinants of the term structure of interest rates. On one view long-term interest rates are said to reflect investors' expectations of what short-term rates will be in future. In so far as this is correct the authorities can best alter the term structure of interest rates by controlling the rediscount rate or by influencing expectations by means, for instance, of the terms on which they issue a new stock. The scale and maturity of their open-market transactions will affect the term structure only indirectly through their influence on investors' expectations.

An alternative view is that the market is segmented, with investors having some preferred habitat in the maturity range: life assurance companies and pension funds prefer long-dated stocks, while banks and discount houses are reluctant to hold stocks which will mature in more than ten years or five years respectively. Investors can be persuaded to hold stock outside of their preferred maturity range only if they are given an adequate price incentive.

This theory implies that the authorities can influence relative interest rates on debts of differing maturities by altering the composition of the central government debt held by the market: sales of long-dated stocks accompanied by purchases of short-dated stocks or treasury bills[1] will tend to raise long-term and reduce short-term interest rates. How far long-term rates can be controlled by this means depends on the readiness of long-term lenders, particularly such financial institutions as pension funds and life assurance companies, to substitute government debt for private-sector debt or equity in their asset portfolios. It depends also on the extent to which private-sector borrowers in the capital market are influenced by the cost of capital, and their willingness

1. Provided these are not treated as part of the reserve base.

to substitute short-term for long-term borrowing in response to changes in relative interest rates thus offsetting the effects of changes in the maturity structure of central government debt. The scope for this is restricted because the private sector is effectively limited to changing the maturity structure of new borrowing, which is small in relation to the outstanding stock of debt capital, while the authorities can operate on a much larger scale.

Whatever view is taken of the scope for influencing relative interest rates through open-market operations a contraction of the reserve base by this means will raise the general level of interest rates and conversely an expansion of the base will lower interest rates. If loans from the central bank form the residual source of funds required by government, the authorities can also influence the size of the reserve base by altering the terms on non-marketable government debt instruments – national savings in the UK. A rise in the rate of interest offered will attract more funds to the government and consequently reduce its reliance on the central bank.[1]

Such a change in interest rates under the authorities' direct control is one example of how they can also influence the general level of interest rates. For the rates offered by financial institutions competing for these funds will also rise – though not necessarily at precisely the same time or by the same amount – in an effort to avoid a diminution in the funds available to them.

The most common direct measure taken by monetary authorities to influence interest rates is a change in the rediscount rate – the rate at which the central bank will rediscount bills proffered by the commercial banks – or the rate charged by the central bank for loans to the commercial banking system. In the UK this is now called the Bank of England's minimum lending rate – formerly it was Bank rate. A rise in this rate makes it more expensive for the commercial banks to augment their reserves on their own initiative by borrowing from or transferring assets to the central bank, and other short-term money rates are usually linked to it. These other rates are of course influenced by the ease or tightness of money, and if in the face of rising market

1. See Chapters 2 and 3 above.

rates the central bank does not raise the rediscount rate, its own control of the reserve base is endangered, since banks will find it profitable to borrow from it. It is therefore a common practice for the central bank to move its rediscount rate in line with movements in market rates. But if the authorities wish to bring about a change in the general level of interest rates they may also alter the rediscount rate autonomously, knowing that market rates will usually follow quickly and that they can maintain the new level by adjusting the size of the reserve base in due course. An autonomous change in the rediscount rate is a signal to the market of the authorities' intention to alter monetary conditions, and creates the expectations that justify a change in the general level of interest rates.

Reserve requirements

It is hardly surprising to find that in contrast with the small number of general instruments of control at the disposal of monetary authorities the number of specific control instruments is comparatively large. Many of these apply mainly to banks – examples are changes in reserve requirements and changes in rediscount quotas – but others may also apply to non-bank financial institutions. Controls on lending to specified categories of borrowers, and compulsory holdings of assets other than reserve assets are examples from this category.

Most central banks stipulate the minimum ratio of reserve assets to deposit liabilities which the commercial banks must hold, and most have the right to vary this ratio. An increase in the required reserve ratio means that banks have to hold more reserves for any given level of deposits, and in the absence of any increase in the supply of reserves, puts pressure on them to reduce their earning assets and thus their deposits. Conversely, a reduction in reserve requirements has an expansionary influence. Reserve requirement variations are therefore seen as an alternative to open-market operations as a technique for influencing the money supply.

There has been considerable controversy over their relative merits in circumstances when both instruments can be regarded as feasible. It is not disputed that in the absence of a well-developed market in government securities or suitable commercial bills, variable reserve requirements should be the preferred means – technical difficulties preclude the carrying out of open-market operations. Nor is there any doubt that open-market operations are the appropriate instrument for offsetting the comparatively small variations in bank reserves which result from day-to-day operations in foreign exchange or other transient factors. Controversy is thus restricted to conditions where there is an adequate market in securities and where the authorities want to bring about a substantial change in bank deposits or in bank lending to the private sector.

The two methods can be regarded as alternatives when the banking system is controlled through a reserve base mechanism and the authorities determine the supply of reserves. Open-market sales of securities by the authorities absorb reserves and thus encourage a contraction in the level of bank deposits, given the ratio of required reserves to deposits which is in force. An increase in reserve requirements raises the demand for the given volume of reserves, and reduces the equilibrium level of deposits which the reserves will support. In practice the link between the level of deposits and the level of reserves is not rigid, and in the short run both means of control have the effect of increasing the cost (explicit or implicit) of reserves, which stimulates an adjustment of bank portfolios towards the new equilibrium. For the purpose of exposition we shall assume, however, that reserve ratios are maintained rigidly and that full adjustment is instantaneous.

Consider a bank – assumed to be typical of the banking system – which is in full equilibrium with balance sheet 1. The required reserve ratio is 10 per cent. Now suppose that the monetary authorities make open-market sales of securities so that reserves fall by 1; with a credit multiplier of 10 this induces a contraction of 10 in deposits. Balance sheet 2 shows a possible equilibrium for the bank after this deposit contraction has taken place: in this example the ratio of loans to securities is approximately the same as in balance sheet 1. The same reduction in deposits could be achieved by increasing the required reserve ratio to 11·1 per cent, thus also reducing the volume of deposits which can be supported by the given amount of reserves to 90.

Consider the position shown in balance sheet 3, in which loans are the same as in balance sheet 2 but the higher reserves are matched by lower securities. Can this be a position of full equilibrium?

Balance Sheet 1

Liabilities		Assets	
Deposits	100	Reserves	10
		Securities	28
		Loans	62

Balance Sheet 2

Liabilities		Assets	
Deposits	90	Reserves	9
		Securities	25
		Loans	56

Balance Sheet 3

Liabilities		Assets	
Deposits	90	Reserves	10
		Securities	24
		Loans	56

Aschheim (1963) asserts that it cannot. Since securities yield more than reserves, balance sheet 3 yields lower profits than balance sheet 2; and, according to Aschheim, since reserves are more liquid than securities it is also more liquid. Now in choosing their portfolios banks balance their desire for profits against their need for liquidity. In equilibrium a reduction in profitability will be associated with less, not more, liquidity. Therefore, says Aschheim, if balance sheet 2 is an equilibrium, balance sheet 3 which offers less profit but more liquidity cannot be; the bank will choose to increase loans at the expense of securities, thereby marginally increasing profits at the cost of a marginal reduction in liquidity. On this view a possible equilibrium is shown in balance sheet 4.

Balance Sheet 4

Liabilities		Assets	
Deposits	90	Reserves	10
		Securities	23
		Loans	57

Aschheim concludes that in this situation open-market operations should be preferred to variations in reserve requirements because bank loans will be cut more. The effect on expenditure of cutting bank loans will presumably be greater than that of selling securities, if only because credit rationing will be more severe. But Aschheim's conclusion is only as good as the reasoning behind it, and this has been challenged by the present author – Bain (1964) – amongst others.

The main issue is whether reserves are necessarily more liquid than securities. This is certainly true of *excess* reserves, if the banks choose to hold any, but it is not true of *required* reserves. Putting aside a contingent need for liquidity in the event of a bank being wound up, banks hold liquid assets for two reasons: to meet a loss of deposits and to meet their customers' legitimate demands for advances. Only a small part of banks' reserves are available to meet a deposit loss because the balance must be held to support the bank's remaining deposits. The bulk of any deposit loss must be met from *excess* reserves, sales of securities or contraction of loans; for example, if the required reserve ratio is 10 per cent and there are no excess reserves 90 per cent of a deposit loss must be met by adjusting earning assets. Moreover, since for the individual bank an increase in loans does not involve a loss of deposits,[1] required reserves make no contribution at all to satisfying this need for liquidity.

In none of the illustrative balance sheets are there any excess reserves. Although reserves in balance sheet 3 are higher than in balance sheet 2, they are all required, and it can be shown that the maximum loss of deposits which can be sustained without either falling below the legal minimum reserves – 10 per cent in situation 2 and 11·1 per cent in situation 3 – or calling in loans

1. For the individual bank an increase in loans does of course involve a reduction in holdings of some other asset.

is less under balance sheet 3 than balance sheet 2. Contrary to Aschheim's assertion, balance sheet 3 is less liquid than balance sheet 2, and since profitability is also less it could conceivably be a full equilibrium position. There is thus no reason to expect that, for any given reduction in deposits, open-market operations will be associated with a greater contraction of loans than reserve requirement variations will be; indeed it can be shown that if banks held sufficient securities to support the same maximum loss of deposits in both cases the reverse would be true.

It seems that this particular approach does not give any good grounds for preferring one type of measure to the other. Is there any other basis for choice? We should note first that a required reserve ratio which is higher than that which the banks regard as appropriate to ensure their own solvency and to maintain the liquidity of their deposits is, in effect, a tax on banks: they are being compelled to hold directly or at one remove low-yielding (or in some cases non-interest-bearing) government debt. An increase in reserve requirements implies an increase in this tax. If it is thought undesirable to increase a tax which falls on one particular group of financial institutions that is a reason for preferring open-market operations which have a much less discriminatory impact; this feeling may partially account for the reluctance of some monetary authorities to increase reserve requirements. In the UK the *special deposits* scheme has the same effect as a variable reserve requirement, but the term implies that these additional deposits (which bear interest at much the same rate as reserve assets) are not supposed to be regarded as a permanent imposition on the banks.

On the other hand, conditions may easily arise, even when there is a well-developed market in securities, in which the monetary authorities would have to sacrifice other objectives if they attempted to contract credit substantially through open-market sales. During a credit squeeze the private sector is not usually willing to absorb large quantities of securities quickly; and if banks and other financial intermediaries were also to appear as sellers in the market, the risk of a disorderly market – in the sense that a sharp, shortly-to-be-reversed, fall in the price of securities occurs – is high if the authorities try to sell any appreciable volume. They may even find themselves reluctantly buying securities in order to prevent a disorderly market. In these circumstances a combination of an *increase* in reserve requirements and open-market *purchases* of securities may permit the authorities to achieve a contraction of credit without disorderly markets – the open-market purchases providing some, but not all, of the cash or liquid assets which the banks need to meet the new level of required reserves.

Even if the authorities do not actively seek to contract private lending by the banks, circumstances may easily arise in which an increase in reserve requirements is the preferred instrument of policy. For instance, if the authorities are faced with a short-term capital inflow from abroad, which automatically builds up the reserve assets in the banks' portfolios, they may neutralize the increase by raising the required reserve ratio.[1] Similarly if heavy deficit financing by the government leads to financing through the banking system the authorities may use an increase in reserve requirements to mop up the banks' excess reserves, and avoid any easing of conditions in private credit markets.

There are other conditions in which monetary policy can be carried out most effectively by reducing reserve requirements. For example, in the USA, if the general credit situation was favourable a large new treasury issue could provide the occasion for a reduction in reserve requirements in order to minimize the short-term impact on interest rates of the new issue. A comparable situation would arise in the UK if heavy sales of gilt-edged stocks by the authorities threatened the banks' liquidity and seemed likely to curtail private lending excessively. By releasing special deposits the authorities would be able to continue selling stocks, thereby lengthening the maturity of the national debt and satisfying the private sector's appetite for stock, without putting pressure on bank lending.[2]

1. In the UK the level of special deposits may differ according to the category of liability. Thus the authorities have the power to stipulate a much higher ratio of special deposits for funds borrowed abroad than for domestic deposits.

2. In the UK uncertainty and unstable expectations concerning future interest rates have led to sharp fluctuations in the institutions' (particularly life assurance and pension funds') purchases of government securities. By

When we recognize that the monetary authorities are not bent simply on achieving one single objective but must consider simultaneously a number of partially conflicting objectives it appears that there is no good reason for consistently preferring either open-market operations or changes in reserve requirements as the main instrument of policy. Although in some circumstances they can both be employed as means of expanding or contracting credit, they are different in their impact on the securities markets and on the profitability of banks. The choice between them, or a decision to use some combination of both, will depend on the authorities' attitude towards these other considerations.

Rediscount quotas

Another arrangement by which the central bank may affect the supply of reserves is the rediscount quota. The central bank fixes a quota for each commercial bank, and is prepared to rediscount eligible commercial bills held by the bank up to the quota limit. Unused rediscount facilities within the quota represent a reliable source of reserves to the bank, reserves which can be obtained on the bank's own initiative. A cut in rediscount quotas serves therefore to curtail the supply of reserve assets on which the banks can count, and conversely for an increase. Banks may be expected to react to the change in supply conditions by adjusting the composition of their asset portfolios and terms of lending in the usual way.

Ceilings and directional controls

In many countries the authorities attempt, through the banking system, to secure finance on favourable terms for certain categories of borrower whilst discouraging lending to others. They may do this by imposing a ceiling on lending to the private sector, thereby discriminating in favour of public bodies, by arranging finance on special terms for some borrowers, or by simply enjoining the banks to lend for some purposes but not for others. They may also limit the interest rate paid by banks for

altering the level of special deposits the authorities can do something to insulate other credit markets from these oscillations.

deposits, thereby protecting the banks' competitors in the market for funds, or place a ceiling on certain liabilities issued by the banks, with penalties for exceeding the ceiling, which has the same effect.

Requests or directives of these kinds have become commonplace in the UK. At their most severe they took the form of a ceiling on each bank's lending to the private sector, related to the actual level of the bank's private-sector advances on some base date. This type of control was applied to banks in Britain for most of the 1960s. Similar requests referred to commercial bill holdings – in an effort to control bank liquidity or to prevent avoidance of the advances ceiling by employing alternative means of finance – and to particular classes of lending, such as advances to hire-purchase finance companies and to property companies. There have also been exhortations to provide finance readily for exports, but not for imports or personal consumption, and there are arrangements to provide export finance at a fixed and relatively cheap rate.

It is difficult to tell how effective these admonitions have been. As far as statistical information has allowed the extent of compliance to be verified it appears that most banks have made some effort to carry out the Bank of England's requests. There have certainly been reductions in lending to persons and to hire-purchase finance companies at times when the banks were asked to discriminate against them. It is not always possible – even for the banks themselves – to identify loans which help to finance exports, and very often the financing of imports cannot be distinguished from other financial demands from companies; so the success of this type of discrimination is an open question. Lending under the special arrangements for export credit grew rapidly: it is clear that the growth of this business, which was relatively unprofitable to the banks, owed much to the Bank of England recommendation.

The ceiling applied to the advances made by individual banks or groups of banks was undoubtedly the most important direct control. Even when the request was addressed to a group of banks, such as the London clearing banks, each individual bank was expected to comply. By means of these requests the Bank of

England was able to prevent an extension of advances for which
the commercial banks had adequate resources and which they
would otherwise have chosen to supply. Unless the frustrated
borrowers found funds elsewhere in the banking sector (when
requests were addressed only to the deposit banks) or outside
it, the Bank's request will have had some impact on private
spending.

But the attainment of this objective in this manner has a significant cost. When a ceiling on lending is in force the main
weapon for competition among the banks and between them and
other financial institutions is blunted. Depositors are attracted
by a bank's willingness and ability to make loans; the possibility
that they may wish to have loans from time to time, and the
bank's willingness to accommodate them, is a powerful influence
on where potential customers choose to keep any spare funds. If
banks are not permitted to make loans to private individuals for
consumption purchases, it is likely that some customers will be
attracted by higher interest rates offered by other financial institutions such as building societies. This type of control therefore
damages the banks' competitive position in relation to other
financial institutions.

It also freezes competition amongst the banks themselves. In
normal conditions each bank manager would consider an application for a loan on its merits in relation to the funds his bank
had available for lending, and an applicant who was unsuccessful
in his application to one bank might frequently be successful at
another. When the banks are constrained by requests competition
cannot operate freely, and a manager would not wish to take on a
customer who had had his application turned down by a com-
petitor solely because the bank wished to comply with the authorities' request. To do otherwise would be to invite customers to
change their banks, each bank gaining some and losing others, to
the benefit of none.

Quite apart from turning down loan applications from existing
customers the banks are unable actively to seek new lending
business – one of the best ways of increasing their share of the
market. Competition between banks is consequently directed into
the provision of services, which may be both an expensive means

of attracting depositors and a relatively inefficient counter to the competition from other financial institutions.

Directional controls, interest-rate ceilings and limits on deposits have similar effects: they distort competition both within the banking sector and between banks and other financial institutions. The distortion may, of course, be intended, as when a ceiling on deposit interest is designed to protect building societies in the UK or savings and loan associations in the USA from an outflow of funds, which would have repercussions on activity in the housing market and perhaps on the political fortunes of the government of the day. But there can also be unintended consequences. In both the UK and the USA direct inter-company lending developed in place of intermediation through the banks, and in the UK the ceiling on interest payable by banks for small deposits seemed to benefit local authorities, which were not restricted in the interest rates they offered, more than the building societies which were the intended beneficiaries. Ceilings therefore are undoubtedly damaging to the competitive strength of the banking industry. The degree of damage suffered depends on the duration of the ceiling and the expansion, if any, of lending which is permitted. The longer a ceiling is in force, and the greater the restraint it imposes, the more damage it does to the normal work of competition in allowing the efficient bank to expand at the expense of the inefficient and the banks as a whole to compete with uncontrolled, or less rigidly controlled, financial institutions. If ceilings are imposed only for a short period when a rapid expansion of private credit would otherwise take place they may do comparatively little damage. But if maintained for a period of years the damage may well be severe. Moreover, their effectiveness in influencing spending is likely to diminish the longer they are in force, as reactions in the rest of the financial system lead to credit flowing through channels which by-pass the banks as financial intermediaries.

Other compulsory asset holdings

In many countries financial institutions, including banks, are required to hold a minimum proportion of certain specified assets, usually some form of government security, in their port-folios. Since government securities are free of commercial risks the regulations may reflect a desire to guarantee the liquidity and solvency of the institutions concerned. Such regulations have the effect, however, of ensuring that a minimum proportion of the new saving which the community chooses to channel through these institutions flows to the government; and in so far as the regulations lead the institutions to increase the proportion of their portfolios held in this form, they reduce the cost of government borrowing.

Compulsory asset holdings affect the competitive position of the institutions concerned, because they cause the institutions to increase their holdings of relatively low-yielding assets. Like required reserves for the banks, they act as a tax. A low tax, spread widely over the institutions, will cause less distortion of competition amongst the institutions than a higher tax which is narrowly concentrated; though the existence of any tax at all provides an incentive to direct transactions between borrowers and lenders, without the intervention of an intermediary.

At certain times the authorities may also require financial institutions to subscribe to new issues of government debt. Just as special deposits made by banks in the UK can be employed to neutralize heavy government borrowing, so such purchases of government debt or compulsory deposits with the central bank can be used for the same purpose elsewhere: they provide the government with funds which would otherwise be borrowed through the banking system and would be reflected in the reserve base.

Control of instalment lending

The power to vary the terms of hire-purchase and other instalment lending contracts is an important weapon of monetary control. In the USA it is held by the Federal Reserve Board, but in Britain the Department of Trade, rather than the monetary authorities, is responsible for these controls. Hire-purchase controls specify the minimum down-payment and the maximum repayment period which are permissible for hire-purchase con-tracts, the detailed regulations varying between different classes of goods. By altering these minimum terms the authorities are able to influence expenditure on the commodities to which the controls apply.

When hire-purchase, controls are tightened it is usual both to raise the minimum down-payment and to shorten the maximum repayment period. The former cuts demand by forcing potential purchasers to save a larger proportion of the price before they acquire the goods. The initial impact may be substantial, but the effect on spending wears off after a time as potential purchasers gradually save up enough to pay the higher down-payment required. Nevertheless, there is likely to be some permanent effect on demand for the controlled commodities, because some potential purchasers will choose to buy other goods which are uncontrolled.

The length of the maximum repayment period determines the minimum amount which a purchaser must be able to pay regularly in order to buy the goods. Suppose that a purchaser of a car wants to borrow £600 – the difference between the price of his new car and the car he is trading in. If the maximum repayment period is thirty months he must be able to afford to repay £20 of capital per month, plus charges. By cutting the repayment period to twenty-four months the authorities can raise the minimum monthly repayment to £25, plus charges. Now in practice many people buying cars, furniture, or other consumer durables decide what monthly payment they can afford and take on hire-purchase contracts which entail this much spending. When the authorities cut the repayment period these purchasers react by buying less expensive or fewer goods. This effect probably lasts longer than the effect from raising down-payments, but it too wears off after a time because people with twenty-four-month contracts are likely to come back into the market sooner than people with thirty-month contracts: the greater frequency of purchase offsets the lower value each time a purchase is made.

There is no doubt that changes in hire-purchase controls can have a substantial impact on saving in the short run. A tightening of terms reduces the total sum outstanding under hire-purchase contracts. Most of this is borrowed by the personal sector and most people who use hire-purchase do not have access to alternative sources of funds. Thus a tightening of hire-purchase terms reduces personal consumption, and since any feedback to personal income is delayed it increases personal saving in the short run. If the authorities wish to increase saving in the short run hire-purchase controls make an effective instrument, which has the great advantage of acting quickly. An easing of hire-purchase controls is also an effective way of stimulating economic activity.

It is doubtful, however, whether hire-purchase controls have any long-term effect on saving. Tight controls are certainly associated with a lower amount of hire-purchase debt outstanding than are easy controls. But borrowing in any period equals the *change* in the level of debt outstanding, and there is no evidence that this will be held back permanently by tight controls. In the long term people will certainly make less use of hire-purchase if controls are tight, but it does not follow that they actually spend less because although it is quite likely that their spending on durables will be held down their spending on other things may well be increased.

In spite of their undoubted short-run effectiveness hire-purchase controls are an unpopular instrument of monetary policy – so much so that the Federal Reserve Board appear to have dispensed with them. The main reason is that their impact is concentrated on a narrow range of industries – motor vehicles, furniture and other consumer durables. The achievement of a substantial effect on the economy as a whole must be very disruptive to these industries. Because their impact is so concentrated hire-purchase controls are seen as a highly discriminatory instrument of monetary policy. Moreover, it is strongly argued by the industries concerned that the disturbances to their plans which result from variations in hire-purchase controls reduce their efficiency.

This line of argument has not prevented considerable use being made of hire-purchase controls in Britain. Official policy may discriminate quite deliberately against personal consumption, and if it does so producers of consumer durable goods will suffer disproportionately whatever the means employed. However, the nature of consumers' reactions to changes in controls – a sharp initial effect which wears off gradually – suggests that several comparatively small changes in controls spread over a period will be less disruptive than one large change.

There are two further objections to hire-purchase controls. The first, which applies equally to any other specific control, is that it invites avoidance and stimulates new channels of finance. In the UK the controls do not technically cover personal loans, and over a wide field these have now replaced pure hire-purchase contracts. In practice, this does not create a loop-hole because the main finance houses and banks have agreed with the Bank of England that similar terms will be applied to these loans. Rental agreements form another means of avoiding hire-purchase controls, but can be regulated by stipulating that a minimum number of payments must be made in advance. However, check trading and other practices have arisen which allow the controls to be avoided. There is no reason to believe that some of those alternatives would be used so widely in the absence of hire-purchase controls; in the long term controls which create inefficiency but do not affect spending must be undesirable.

The other objection is that the controls are very difficult to enforce. One aspect of this is illustrated in the previous paragraph, but even if no alternative means of finance existed trading practices can make enforcement almost impossible. When a used car is traded-in against the purchase of a newer car the purchaser is concerned only with the difference in price. The trade-in usually forms the down-payment for a hire-purchase agreement. The percentage down-payment can be raised by inflating the trade-in allowance and the purchase price of the new car by the same amount. While there are limits to this practice there is clearly considerable scope for it when one used car is being traded-in and another purchased. The same effect is achieved in other consumer durables, such as washing machines, when prices are inflated but an excessive allowance is made for an old washing machine traded-in.

We can summarize by saying that hire-purchase controls can be an effective instrument for short-term economic management. But there is a danger of causing excessive disruption to a narrow range of industry, and if controls are maintained for long they will be avoided and cause inefficiency.

Margin requirements

One further policy instrument, which is available to the Federal Reserve Board but has no British counterpart, is the margin requirement. Regulation of the stock-market through margin requirements is intended to minimize the chance of speculative booms followed by a collapse of credit, such as occurred in and after 1929 in America. Speculative stock-market booms exaggerate any inherent instability in the economy.

The margin requirement states the minimum proportion of the cost of a security which the purchaser must provide from his own funds, the balance being borrowed from a bank or broker. For example, when the required margin is 60 per cent the bank is not permitted to lend more than 40 per cent of the amount needed to purchase a security. Now rising stock-market prices increase the owner's capital and, with a constant percentage margin, would allow him to increase his borrowing. Suppose, for example, that an investor buys stock worth $5000 initially, using $3000 of his own funds and $2000 of borrowed funds; his margin initially is 60 per cent. If the stock price doubles to $10,000 the value of his equity becomes $8000, and this allows him to borrow another $3000 to buy more stock without falling short of the margin required. Consequently, so long as lenders are willing to supply the additional funds a stock-market boom can proceed unchecked as purchasers with newly borrowed funds drive prices ever higher – unless the Federal Reserve Board increase the margin requirements. In the example cited an increase in the margin requirement from 60 per cent to 80 per cent would offset the effect of the higher stock price and leave the investor's ability to borrow unchanged.

Conclusion

In the long run the instruments of monetary control which impinge mainly on particular groups of financial institutions or particular types of transaction distort the free working of the economic system and cause some inefficiency. Within highly developed financial systems measures which are applied over only a narrow range of financial institutions may even be self-defeating: capital and credit flows will find other channels which are not impeded. There is therefore a presumption in favour of general as opposed to specific measures of control as the means of exerting a continuous influence on financial activity.

It must be expected, however, that from time to time there may be large shifts in the demand for capital funds without any corresponding shift in supply. On these occasions, if the authorities attempted to maintain balance in the economy entirely through non-specific instruments of control such as open-market operations and changes in explicit interest rates, they might have to act with a vigour which would involve sacrificing other important policy objectives. It would then be appropriate to re-inforce non-specific measures with other control instruments which affect particular institutions and which make it possible to achieve balance in the capital and credit markets more easily.

There is no general presumption that open-market operations will be more effective than variations in reserve requirements as a means of influencing bank lending: the choice between these instruments will depend on the circumstances in which they are to be applied. Ceilings on lending by banks and other financial institutions, and controls on hire-purchase terms, may be useful in an emergency and may affect spending quickly but will certainly damage the efficiency of the financial system if retained for long periods. Compulsory asset holdings by a wide range of institutions interfere much less with competition. But there is the danger that if they are set too high they will constitute a tax on financial intermediation which will inhibit activity in the capital market. Finally, margin requirements improve stability and requests and other forms of guidance on the terms and direction of lending may be useful in the short term. In the longer term they must be regarded as disguised taxes (on prohibited borrowers) or subsidies (to preferred borrowers) and can be justified only if the implied subsidies can be justified and if the means of financing them seems desirable.

8   Monetary Targets and Indicators

The role of monetary policy in economic management

The role which governments assign to monetary policy reflects the priority given to various policy objectives and is determined in conjunction with decisions taken about other policy instruments. Monetary policy is thus only one component of the machinery through which governments seek to influence their countries' economies. Together with fiscal policy it bears the brunt of demand management, though other aspects of policy such as labour legislation and the control of business enterprises are also involved. Monetary policy is also important for the allocation of resources between, for example, large and small firms, investment and consumption, or residential construction and investment in plant and equipment. But, as we have already seen in Chapter 2, whatever their domestic objectives may be, the monetary authorities in countries linked by fixed exchange rates are strongly influenced by the actions of their partners, and these links restrict the ability of any single country to follow an independent course.

In carrying out monetary policy the authorities attempt to attain their *objectives* by influencing certain *targets* of policy – interest rates or monetary aggregates which they can hope to influence and which relate to their objectives. They also need some means of ascertaining what is the actual stance of policy, whether it is contractionary or expansionary, and they do this by observing *indicators*, again usually interest rates or monetary aggregates. We shall now consider the nature of these objectives, targets and indicators.

Objectives of monetary policy

The objectives of government economic policy may be summarized as a satisfactory rate of growth in real *per capita* income, a high average level of employment, the avoidance of unnecessary fluctuations in income and employment, the maintenance of approximate balance between foreign payments and receipts without recourse to borrowing, and stability of prices. In the short run these are all seen as objectives, but in the long run price stability and balance in foreign payments are usually regarded as constraints which influence the extent to which other objectives can be achieved rather than as objectives in themselves, and most governments are in fact willing to allow a moderate price inflation if this permits them to achieve other objectives. In the short run it is evident that balance in foreign payments is not a constraint, and the effect which monetary actions will have on short-term capital flows to or from other countries is an important consideration in the determination of monetary policy. The authorities may choose to keep interest rates above the level generally ruling elsewhere in order to encourage an inflow (or discourage an outflow) of short-term capital at a time when a balance-of-payments deficit on current and long-term capital account has to be financed; or they may reduce interest rates to discourage short-term capital inflows which would merely add to a surplus.

Since the factors which contribute towards a high rate of economic growth are by no means fully understood it is difficult to say anything definite on the subject of monetary policy and economic growth. In a world in which the monetary authorities control the real rate of interest monetary policy may influence growth through its effect on the level of investment. Suppose that the authorities set monetary and fiscal policy so that together they maintain some given level of economic activity. Other things being equal, the less restrictive is monetary policy, i.e. the lower are interest rates and the easier is credit, and the more restrictive is fiscal policy, the higher will be the level of investment. (This might not follow if particular fiscal measures aimed directly at stimulating investment were offset against a tighter monetary policy, but it is likely to be true if all taxes or government expenditure were simply adjusted proportionally in order to maintain balance.) The higher investment promotes economic growth: it allows a permanent increase in the rate at which potential improvements in techniques are embodied in capital equipment, and growth is also accelerated for a period (which may be measured in decades) during which the economy moves from an equilibrium in which capital-intensity is relatively low to one in which capital-intensity is higher.

In helping to maintain stability of income and prices monetary policy may also contribute towards growth. It is not at all clear whether a very high level of capacity utilization is more or less conducive to rapid growth than a slightly lower level, but it is certain that deep depressions are bad for growth. By moderating economic fluctuations so that depressions are avoided monetary policy makes it easier for governments to achieve their growth objectives. Similarly, while the effect of moderate or steady price changes on growth is uncertain, we do know that rapid and variable rates of inflation discourage investment by undermining the basis on which future plans can be made, and that hyper-inflation leading ultimately to the breakdown of the monetary economy is undoubtedly bad for growth.

The authorities may also be concerned about the way in which monetary tightness affects particular groups of borrowers and particular classes of investment more than others. Tight credit affects small firms more than large, and high interest rates appear to have a greater impact on investment in housing and, in the USA, state and local construction than on industrial and commercial investment. This may pose problems for governments if the resulting distribution of investment does not correspond to their own priorities.

In the rest of this chapter we shall assume that there is sufficient exchange-rate flexibility to allow the monetary authorities in any country some independence of action; and while acknowledging the long-run connection between persistent monetary expansion and prices, we shall be concerned with the short run in which economic activity as well as prices may be influenced. We shall therefore consider monetary policy in the context of counter-cyclical economic policy.

Targets of monetary policy

In this context monetary policy acts as an adjunct of fiscal policy in maintaining stability of income and employment. Fiscal policy is often given the leading role, with major changes usually taking place once a year when government expenditure and taxation are determined for the ensuing year. The main consideration in deciding upon changes in the general level of taxation is the government's desire to adjust the prospective level of activity in the economy to some target level. An increase in the government surplus (or decrease in the deficit) tends to reduce the level of economic activity: in terms of the usual Keynesian analysis injections into the income stream are reduced or absorptions from it are increased.

Governments make their budget judgements on the basis of economic forecasts which are usually built up from forecasts of the major autonomous components of spending – exports, private investment, known public-spending programmes – which are thought to be largely independent of the current level of activity, together with estimates of endogenous elements in demand – personal consumption, stock-building, imports – which are expected to vary with the level of activity actually achieved. The latter involve estimates of the propensity to save, the relation between stock-building and other components of demand, and the propensity to import, which are derived from econometric studies of some parts of the structure of the economy (see McMahon, 1965, for a description of practice in Britain at that time).

If the forecasts of the exogenous elements of final demand were known with precision and were unaffected by monetary conditions, and if the structural relations in the economy determining the levels of the endogenous components were also well understood and fixed there would be nothing for monetary policy to do in stabilizing the economy: the government could achieve whatever level of demand, and hence activity, it desired simply by adjusting fiscal policy. Monetary policy enters the picture because some of the exogenous components of demand are influenced by monetary policy, because monetary variables appear as arguments in the structual relations which link the exogenous and endogenous variables and because the forecasts of the exogenous components of demand and estimates of the structural relations are not at all certain. With these sources of error present some policy instrument which can be adjusted frequently is required. The adjustments made through fiscal policy are usually comparatively large and infrequent: monetary policy, which can change rapidly and by large or small degrees, offers a more flexible tool for maintaining balance in the periods between changes in fiscal measures.

The choice of target for monetary policy is determined by the view taken of the mechanism through which money influences the economy. This has already been discussed in Chapter 6. A target should play a key role in the transmission mechanism, and policy can be effective only if both the influence of the instruments of monetary policy – the levers which the authorities control – on the target and the impact of the target on the authorities' objectives are understood.

For the monetarist, the money supply itself is the obvious choice as target variable. The behaviour of the money supply can be controlled by operating on the high-powered money base, and changes in the money stock are thought to have a predictable effect on economic activity and prices. However, matters are not altogether clear-cut. A choice must be made from amongst the alternative measures of money available, and although the relationships between money (however defined) and income seem to be fairly reliable in the long run, behaviour in the short term is rather erratic. Indeed, monetarists generally conclude that the authorities should not attempt to carry out a counter-cyclical monetary policy because uncertainty, lags in the effect of measures, and political pressures to take excessive action all combine to create the danger that policy will destabilize rather than stabilize the economy. It is suggested therefore that the authorities should adopt some rule for monetary expansion and seek to make the money supply target grow steadily at this rate.

In contrast, the Keynesian view of the transmission mechanism suggests that interest rates and the availability of credit should be treated as targets. In the short run the authorities can influence interest rates and by rationing or other means they can also alter other credit conditions, which are linked in turn to economic activity. But, as we shall see, interest-rates targets and others closely connected with interest rates are also open to criticism.

Much of the theoretical work on financial markets has been developed under the aegis of Professor Tobin at Yale University, e.g. Tobin (1969). Tobin urges that the market yield on equity should be chosen as the target for monetary policy. The authorities should try to equate this yield with the real return expected from investment in physical capital. When the real rate of return on equity rises, the value of existing capital equipment falls and discourages the purchase of new capital equipment; in the reverse situation investment is stimulated when the cost of production of new capital is less than its market value. The key to controlling the rate of investment is consequently the control of the real return on equity, and 'the valuation of investment goods relative to their cost is the prime indicator and proper target of monetary policy' (Brainard and Tobin, 1968, p. 104).

Brainard and Tobin recognize, of course, that in practice there are many markets for physical capital, e.g. the housing market as well as the market for equities, and that as a result more than one comparison must be kept in view. But they argue forcefully that this type of comparison is crucial and that no other target, whether some nominal interest rate or some aggregate of financial assets, will do as well because shocks to the system, emanating either from changes in asset preferences or from changes in the income–expenditure side, will frequently distort the relationship between the key variables and any other targets.

This type of target has many attractions. The market value of equity capital can be observed easily and an index of market value can be compared with a price index for investment goods. A rise in the former relative to the latter indicates a movement towards greater investment. Similarly, in the housing market price indices of existing houses and of new building costs can easily be constructed. But there are some difficulties. It is not at all easy to see what target would be appropriate in the market for some consumer durables or other instances in which there is only a very imperfect market in existing capital. And even in the equity market it is by no means clear that the purchasers of newly-produced capital goods share the expectations of the majority of asset-holders in the financial markets. The validity of the Tobin–Brainard target depends on changes in financial investors' expectations being mirrored by changes in industrialists' expectations of future profitability. It is quite possible that this is a tolerable approximation to the truth in conditions other than those which prevail towards the peaks and troughs of stock-market cycles. In such circumstances it is often difficult to account for the level of stock-market prices in terms of a rational view of future profitability; changes in stock-market prices are then linked to the building up or liquidation of speculative positions which have little to do with the 'fundamental' value of shares. And it is precisely at these times that it may be most important to adjust monetary policy in attempting to maintain the balance of the economy in the face of sudden and sizeable shifts in the investment demand function.

It is clear that comparisons of the values of existing assets with those of newly produced assets may tell us a lot about changes in the stimulus to invest. But there are gaps and the possibility of severe distortions in this source of information, and the authorities would be unwise to adopt this type of comparison as the sole target of monetary policy.

There are a number of difficulties in using more conventional interest-rate measures as targets. First, while the evidence supports the hypothesis that interest rates and the supply of credit influence spending, we cannot be at all sure about the size and timing of the reaction to any change in these financial conditions. Secondly, so far as interest rates are concerned it is certainly the expected *real* rate of interest which matters, not the nominal rate of interest. While the authorities can both observe and control the nominal rate of interest on bills and bonds they cannot observe the real rate because there is no known measure of the expected rate of price inflation – something which varies from time to time and from person to person. Other things being equal, a rise in nominal rates of interest engineered by the authorities will raise real rates of interest. But other things are often not equal, and the conditions in which the monetary authorities raise money interest rates are often conditions in which expectations of price inflation are growing. During such periods a rise in the nominal rate of interest may well be associated with a fall in the expected real rate. Consequently, the level of nominal interest rates is not a good target for monetary policy.

Changes in the availability of credit may be linked with interest-rate targets because they operate by sharply raising the interest rates facing marginal borrowers. However it is difficult to use credit availability as a target because of the great uncertainty of the extent to which a reduction in the availability of credit through particular institutions will be offset by credit flows through other institutions or direct from lender to borrower; a tightening of credit will have some effect, but it is difficult to predict the amount precisely.

As a generalization we might conclude that the authorities would be well advised not to rely on any one single target but to select their targets according to the prevailing economic and financial conditions. In particular, if the general price level is stable, and in the short run, interest rate targets are suitable; but in the longer run and in times of inflation the authorities should seek to keep the growth of the money supply within narrow bounds.

Indicators of monetary policy

Those financial aggregates or interest rates which serve as targets may also be employed as indicators of monetary policy, expansionary policy being reflected in rapid monetary growth or a fall in interest rates. But other aggregates or interest rates may also be suitable as indicators, whose function is to tell the authorities what is happening, and which do not for this purpose need to be under their control. However, all the difficulties that beset the use of any single measure as a target apply with equal force to indicators.

The justification for employing financial aggregates as indicators of the state of balance in the economy is that variations in liquid assets are a consequence of unanticipated discrepancies between receipts and spending. We have already discussed the notion of a transactions demand for cash, and it can be extended to a wider group of financial assets. Cash, deposit balances of all sorts and short-term money market assets all fulfil this function. The total value of the assets held for this purpose in the economy will be determined in a manner similar to that of the transactions demand for money.

Financial assets are also employed by savers as a home for long-term savings – savings which are either held primarily as a source of income or to meet some foreseeable expenditure in the relatively distant future. Life assurance policies, accrued pension rights, and portfolios of equity shares and long-term bonds are held primarily for this purpose. We shall designate this type of asset a *long-term* asset, and distinguish this group from the other group of *liquid* assets. In practice the dividing line between the two groups is arbitrary.

Unfortunately it is not possible to say that all holdings of one particular group of assets are held as long-term savings and others as short-term balances. In the course of managing a portfolio, asset holders may switch temporarily into liquid assets to take advantage of some expected interest-rate movement, and they may choose to hold some funds permanently in liquid assets to provide themselves with a contingency reserve. Indeed, as total financial asset holdings rise it is reasonable to expect some part of the increase to be held permanently in liquid assets. Nevertheless, even if it is impossible to identify any group of assets uniquely with long-run holdings, it is surely possible to say that temporary accumulations of funds are much more likely to be held in liquid forms – cash, bank deposits, short-term loans to local authorities – than in equities or life assurance policies.

We can relate long-term assets and liquid assets to permanent and transitory savings in consumption theory (see Friedman, 1957). Transitory savings are likely to be held in liquid assets; the bulk of permanent savings will go into long-term assets but part will be held in liquid assets. If we could predict how much of permanent savings would be in liquid assets as a group or in some specific type of liquid asset we could use the observed change in the liquid asset or assets as an indicator of the extent to which current saving was permanent.

Consider the behaviour of the money supply – one particular group of liquid assets. A knowledge of the equilibrium relationship between GNP and the demand for money and of the effect of any changes in relative interest rates on the demand for money would allow us to predict what change in M was warranted by any given change in GNP. Such a change would represent the effect of permanent savings; it would be that part of permanent savings which asset holders choose to hold as money. Any discrepancy between this and the actual change in M would be a sign of imbalance between investment demand and permanent savings; an excess of M above the predicted level would imply that liquid funds were being built up temporarily with transitory savings, because *ex ante* investment exceeded *ex ante* saving, while an unexpectedly small rise in M would mean that permanent savings exceeded investment, i.e. transitory savings were negative.[1]

This is not to assert, of course, that the *whole* of any transitory component in savings will show up in M. It is very likely that some temporary accumulations of funds will be held in forms other than money, and it is possible that the bulk will be held in other forms, especially by holders such as large industrial companies. However, it would be surprising if no part of an imbalance between permanent saving and investment appeared as an unexpected change in money holdings. The behaviour of the money stock, after allowing for the effect of changes in interest rates, is likely to be an indicator of the state of balance in the economy.

This line of argument suggests that no single definition of M will necessarily provide a better indicator than any other. How

1. This analysis is oversimplified because it does not allow for lagged adjustments in the demand for money. Reductions in the money holdings of some asset-holders, whose balances had been temporarily high, may offset the increase in holdings which are being built up out of transitory savings. The 'equilibrium' demand for money should therefore be derived from a dynamic model. Fortunately distortion from lagged adjustments is least likely when monetary action is most important, i.e. when temporary holdings of liquid funds are being accumulated during the upswing of the cycle.

asset holders choose to accumulate any liquid balances will depend on the relative interest rates obtainable on different liquid assets. Provided the demand function for a group of assets is known, that group can serve as an indicator.

Since no demand function is known with precision one cannot expect to be able to say for certain exactly how much of a change in the money stock – or in any other similar indicator – would correspond to a balance between permanent savings and investment. But one could expect to specify upper and lower limits within which the change should lie. If the indicator fell between these limits one could not be sure that permanent savings and investment were in balance; but if the indicator fell outside the range one could be certain that some imbalance existed. For example, suppose that a 5 per cent growth in GNP at current prices would be consistent with a rise in the equilibrium demand for money of between 2 per cent and 6 per cent with a given structure of relative interest rates. If the money stock is observed to grow at an annual rate of 8 per cent it implies that investment is running ahead of savings – it indicates that monetary policy is not maintaining balance between permanent savings and investment.

How should the monetary authorities react to such a situation? Assuming that their objective is steady growth in the economy, they should take steps to alter rates of interest[1] or the reserve base of the banking system until the rate of growth of money returns to an acceptable figure. This will show that interest rates have risen sufficiently to bring investment and permanent savings back into tolerable balance.

At this point it is necessary to add one qualification. To be useful as an indicator any aggregate – whether the money stock or some other group of liquid assets – must have a stable and identifiable demand function. New or discriminatory methods of controlling financial institutions are liable to alter some of the institutional conditions which *implicitly* determine estimated demand functions, and so greatly reduce the value of monetary indicators. The effect of the Federal Reserve Board's

1. Which may in turn alter the acceptable range for the rate of growth of the money stock.

regulation Q, which places an upper limit on the rate of interest payable on time deposits by commercial banks in the USA, illustrates this. When the general level of interest rates rose in 1969 commercial banks were placed at a disadvantage in competing for funds and found difficulty in satisfying their customers' demands for loans. As a result there was a rapid increase in an alternative debt instrument, commercial paper, which carries a higher rate of interest than bank deposits, and which enables companies to borrow funds directly from other companies with funds to spare. This disintermediation process, in which credit flows by-passed the usual financial intermediaries, was associated with a reduction in the demand for money. But there was no way of telling by how much the demand for money had been affected and the value of the money supply as an indicator was greatly reduced. In Britain, direct controls on bank lending also distorted the rate of monetary growth, with similar implications. The use of any particular group of assets as an indicator does depend on the institutions which create these assets being free from discriminatory controls which have an unpredictable effect.

Another possible indicator of imbalance between the permanent savings and investment flows in the economy is a sharp change in the total funds flowing from ultimate lenders to ultimate borrowers. The patterns of financial flows which are likely to be associated with forecast economic developments can be predicted, and any changes in the total flows suggest that the economy is not moving closely in line with the forecast. For example, if the total flow was considerably larger than anticipated this would mean that both borrowing and lending were high, and in the absence of any evidence that the extra financial assets acquired by lenders were intended to be held permanently would imply that permanent saving was running below investment.

There are two difficulties with this indicator. The first is that much less is known about equilibrium flows of funds than about some other aggregates, e.g. money, which may be used as indicators. This makes it very difficult both to predict the total flows which are consistent with forecast economic developments and to appraise the importance of deviations from the prediction. The second is that data on total flows are not usually compiled immediately, and it may well be possible to base decisions on current information which is more readily available.

The last indicator we shall consider is Domestic Credit Expansion (DCE). This is an attempt to generalize the money supply indicator to the conditions which prevail in an open economy. In such an economy *ex post* balance between savings and investment may be associated with involuntary net foreign investment (or disinvestment) – a surplus (or deficit) in the balance of payments. Whereas in a closed economy any imbalance between investment and permanent savings is likely to have some impact on the money supply and accumulations of other liquid assets, in an open economy there may also, or alternatively, be a change in the balance of payments. In broad terms DCE is the sum of the *increase* in the money supply plus the *deficit* in the balance of payments[1] – an imbalance between savings and investment may appear either as credit expansion or as borrowing from abroad. DCE may also be used as a target, and in an open economy it is preferable to a money supply target. A DCE target may be specified by the International Monetary Fund as a condition of assistance to countries which are experiencing severe balance of payments difficulties.

Whether used as a target or indicator DCE has the same merits, and suffers from the same defects, as the money supply. It is probably most useful as part of a major stabilization programme, when a sharp change in the trend of credit expansion is required. It is less suitable in more stable conditions when it may be affected by erratic changes in the demand for bank credit. If a DCE target is adopted and if the authorities choose to use general methods of control – raising or lowering the general level of interest rates – to control DCE there will be little change in the broad pattern of financial flows and DCE will be valuable. On the other hand, it would clearly be possible to take dis-

1. The use of DCE as an indicator in the UK is discussed in Central Statistical Office (1969), *Bank of England Quarterly Bulletin* (1969), and Artis and Nobay (1969).

criminatory measures against the banks which would lower DCE but would have little effect on economic activity because alternative means of finance would be stimulated.

9 The Role of Monetary Policy

In the last fifty years informed opinion on the part which monetary policy should play in economic management has undergone several changes. During the 1920s monetary policy was generally thought to be capable of ironing out fluctuations in economic activity, and the policy of what is now called 'fine tuning' was advocated; credit conditions should be eased in recessions and tightened in booms. However, the economic traumas of the 1930s called the efficacy of monetary policy into question and opinion swung to the other extreme; monetary policy was regarded as powerless to influence the economy in a recession. In the aftermath of the Second World War, thanks to the general scepticism concerning its ability to influence economic activity, monetary policy was for a time deployed for another objective – to raise and then maintain the value of government bonds so that governments could obtain cheap finance. Although by the mid 1950s this particular objective had been abandoned, neither the Radcliffe Committee (1959) in Britain nor the Commission on Money and Credit (1961) in the USA recommended a very active role for monetary policy. More recently, opinion has moved back to a more interventionist position, though some economists, led by Friedman, argue that the swing has gone too far. We shall therefore consider the positions taken by the Radcliffe Committee and by Friedman before putting forward an alternative view.

The Radcliffe Committee view

At the end of its study of the working of the monetary system in the UK the Radcliffe Committee reached the conclusion that monetary policy might properly perform two functions, a background function and an emergency function. Business investment, whether in stocks or in fixed capital, was thought to be insensitive to changes in short-term interest rates, but investment decisions did take some account of the expected cost of long-term funds. Hence long-term rates of interest influenced the balance between saving and investment in the economy. The Committee argued that it would be undesirable to cause long-term rates of interest to fluctuate sharply, since this might undermine the strength and stability of financial institutions, at least so long as they were accustomed to stable interest rates and planned their policies accordingly. Moreover, the time which elapsed between changes in financial conditions and in expenditure on goods and services subsequently seemed to make interest rate policy unsuitable for demand management in the short run. The main duty of the monetary authorities was therefore to try to hold long-term interest rates at the level which would maintain approximate balance between saving and investment in the economy.

While stability of long-term interest rates was deemed desirable, pegging at a constant level went too far because this would have the effect of making all debt equally liquid: if the possibility of capital loss from holding bonds was ruled out, bond-holders would believe that they had ready access to money, and although the Committee did not think that money *per se* was of special importance they did believe that the liquidity of the economy as a whole affected expenditure. Nevertheless, in spite of their view that liquidity mattered for expenditure, the Committee were clearly of the opinion that the level of interest rates, and not any monetary or liquidity aggregate, must be the target for monetary policy.

The Committee also suggested that there was a role for monetary policy in emergency situations, of either a severely deflationary or severely inflationary character. If an emergency situation did arise, they took the view that a package containing both monetary and fiscal measures would be appropriate. Echoing earlier opinions, they did not see much potential for monetary measures in a slump, apart from the removal of any credit controls which might be in operation and from a possible effect of lower long-term rates of interest on house-building activity. They noted too that any attempt to raise the economy from a slump quickly through monetary measures carried a danger for the future, in that the financial system would be flooded with liquidity, and this would be very difficult to control later when business activity was expanding. At the other extreme the Committee also regarded a threat of headlong inflation as an 'emergency'. To deal with such a situation the Committee rejected any restriction on the supply of money itself, but advocated measures to strike more directly and rapidly at the liquidity of spenders. Thus they recommended a combination of controls on capital issues, bank advances and consumer credit. It is noteworthy that all these measures were intended to bear upon aggregate demand, and the Committee did not propose measures to influence wage or other production costs directly.

Severe restrictions on short-term international capital flows existed in most countries in the 1950s and nobody anticipated the rapid growth and immense size of the pool of international capital which now exists. Thus, while the Radcliffe Committee paid some attention to overseas considerations, particularly to the need for adequate reserves of gold and foreign exchange, they did not expect international considerations to govern domestic monetary policy, other than in a balance of payments crisis.

The general impression left by the Radcliffe Committee's report was that monetary policy was not well suited for short-run economic management, which would be better left to fiscal policy. The Commission on Money and Credit, which reported shortly afterwards in the USA, also emphasized the interconnection of fiscal and monetary policy, though in comparison with the Radcliffe Committee they tended to allot a larger role to monetary policy, including direct controls of various kinds in boom conditions.

Friedman and monetary policy

The belief that monetary policy has comparatively little influence on economic stability has gradually lost ground, with the practical consequence that monetary policy has come to play a larger part in economic stabilization programmes. In many countries stabilization policy has not been very successful, partly because when monetary (and also fiscal) measures have been taken it has often been too late and the measures have been excessive. It has therefore been suggested that policies intended to moderate the amplitude of business cycles may in fact have accentuated them. In Friedman's view the inherent dangers are so great, and the probability of avoiding them is so small, that the authorities should voluntarily renounce the use of discretionary monetary policy for stabilization purposes; instead they should adopt a rule of stable monetary growth, at a rate which would be consistent with approximate price stability in the economy, and should not allow the growth of the money supply to depart significantly from this rate.

In his presidential address to the American Economic Association Friedman (1968) sets out the basis for his conclusions. He argues that there are certain objectives which monetary policy cannot conceivably attain – the pegging of interest rates and the fixing of the level of unemployment. Any attempt to achieve these objectives is bound to fail.

Friedman distinguishes sharply between the nominal rate of interest and the real rate of interest, the latter being the nominal rate corrected for the expected rate of price inflation. The equilibrium real rate of interest in the economy is determined by the preferences of savers and the opportunities for investment, not by monetary conditions, and there will be a tendency for the actual real rate of interest to tend towards this equilibrium rate. Friedman acknowledges that in the short run an increase in the rate of growth of the money supply will reduce interest rates. But the stimulus to demand will lead to higher prices and output, thus increasing the demand for money and reducing the real value of the public's cash balances. So the interest rate will rise and, after a time, it will return to its original level – unless in the meantime the experience of rising prices has led to an expectation of further price increases, in which case the nominal rate of interest will rise even further to take account of the expected price inflation. The adjustment for anticipated inflation is likely to be rather slow if the rise in prices has been modest, but people learn from experience and anticipations may adjust very quickly when prices are rising fast. In consequence, any attempt to hold the real rate of interest permanently below its equilibrium level is doomed to failure, because it can only result in accelerating price inflation with concomitant rises in the nominal rate of interest.

The argument concerning the level of unemployment is similar. Easy money may raise employment temporarily, with prices rising faster than wages. But workers are interested in their real wages and, unless they are prepared to accept a reduction, wage bargains will eventually take account of anticipated inflation so that the 'natural' rate of unemployment will be re-established. On the other tack, a tight monetary policy which reduces inflationary price rises will be associated with a rise in unemployment, because wages will keep on rising for some time after prices have begun to slow down, and the real wage can be adjusted down to its equilibrium level only gradually.

It will be observed that, while he asserts that the monetary authorities cannot *peg* the rate of interest or the level of unemployment, Friedman in no way suggests that they are unable to exert an influence in the short run. What he argues is that the equilibrium levels of both are independent of monetary conditions and that, whatever the stance of monetary policy, forces within the economy will tend to drive them back towards these levels. His general conclusion is that the monetary authority can control only nominal quantities, such as the price level, and that it does not have the power to peg any real variables. Furthermore, he suggests that the authorities cannot even select the 'natural' or equilibrium rate of interest or 'natural' level of unemployment as target variables, because they have no means of knowing precisely what these levels are.

What then should the authorities attempt to achieve through monetary policy? First, they should seek to ensure that money itself is not allowed to be a major source of economic disturbance. They should support the strength and stability of the financial system, and if a confidence crisis should arise they should ensure that the quantity of money is not allowed to contract sharply. Secondly, they should provide a stable background for the economy by attempting to keep average prices more or less level;

in this way changes in relative prices would be enabled to carry out their allocative function, without the distortions and uncertainties which are introduced by rapid price inflation. Thirdly, the authorities should offset *major* disturbances from other sources, for example a boom created by postwar expansion or by an explosive government budget. But, as we have already indicated, the authorities should *not* attempt to offset minor disturbances because they are difficult to recognize, their effects cannot be predicted precisely, and it is impossible to judge exactly what the effects of any compensatory monetary measures would be.

Friedman then concludes that the monetary authorities should seek to control monetary aggregates, with the object of providing a stable background to price level, and should avoid sharp swings in policy. A monetary aggregate, rather than the price level itself, should be chosen as the target of policy because while prices are influenced by monetary policy they are not directly controllable. Friedman also ruled out any international objective for monetary policy in the USA, because foreign trade accounted for only a small proportion of national income and in his opinion exchange rate adjustments were the appropriate means of dealing with any imbalances.

An alternative view

There are many countries where international trade and payments are of much greater importance than in the USA, and the theoretical arguments in favour of freely flexible exchange rates have not been fully accepted by governments; instead, although fixed exchange rates are no longer the rule, most governments intervene in the foreign exchange market. Governments see a danger that exchange rate fluctuations will create a climate of uncertainty, damaging both to international trade and economic welfare, and that the exchange rate may exhibit dynamic instability, with a fall in the rate having cumulative effects through its impact on domestic costs and prices. In these circumstances, governments see the maintenance of the foreign exchange value of their currencies as a major objective of monetary policy. Where a currency is widely held internationally, and where there are few barriers to short-term international capital flows – as is the case in the U K – this particular objective of monetary policy limits the scope for using monetary policy as an instrument of domestic economic stabilization. Short-term interest rates in the domestic market cannot be allowed to depart very far from international levels; indeed any attempt to force them apart would automatically be negated by short-term capital flows. Nevertheless, while international considerations *limit* the scope for domestic monetary policy, they do not *eliminate* it entirely.

Even if, as Friedman has argued, monetary policy cannot permanently affect the rate of interest or the level of employment, it can do so temporarily. Forecasts of the future course of economic activity are made at regular intervals, and it is unrealistic to suppose that governments will not attempt either to counter what they see as an undesirable trend in activity or to stimulate a desired trend. Moreover, even if Friedman's advice that the authorities should voluntarily renounce the use of monetary policy as a counter-cyclical instrument might be justified in stable economic conditions, it is more difficult to defend when conditions are already disturbed. Friedman accepts that monetary policy can be used to counter major disturbances. The distinction between a major and a minor disturbance is a fine one, and political pressures seem to make it inevitable that the authorities will attempt to carry out a stabilization purpose wherever they believe they have the power to do so.

It is important that when monetary policy is used in a counter-cyclical role it should be used cautiously. The authorities must allow for the fact that the effects of policy take time to emerge, and that their magnitude is uncertain. They should observe that, since the scope for changing real income is comparatively slight, the *cumulative* effects of substantial monetary growth will be reflected largely in prices. And since the demand for money is roughly proportionate to nominal income, if price inflation is to be avoided a period of rapid monetary growth must be compensated by slow growth later. With its main effect upon prices rather than economic activity, the role of monetary policy in the medium term must be to influence prices.

Rapid changes in the rate of growth of money are associated with changes in both effective demand and real wages. If the economy has adjusted to a rapid rate of inflation the cost of slowing it down sharply may be high. If the growth of the money stock is reined back quickly, effective demand will be cut while real wages rise, thus creating a danger of heavy unemployment. Similarly, if a rapid acceleration of the money stock takes place in a recession there are likely to be sharp, erratic and unintended changes in the distribution of real income. Thus, when the economic system has become adjusted to some particular rate of growth of the money stock, any changes in monetary policy should be gradual.

This does not mean that sharp changes in monetary growth should never be attempted. The economy does not adjust immediately to changes in trend, and the authorities should not be afraid to compensate for earlier errors, before these have been fully incorporated in the economic system. More specifically, if a period of rapid monetary growth has not yet been fully reflected in prices, the authorities may be able to avoid part of the price rise by cutting back monetary growth sharply rather than merely slowing it down gradually.

In summary, in the absence of freely fluctuating exchange rates, monetary policy has an important role to play in implementing the authorities' exchange-rate policy. In so far as an independent domestic monetary policy is feasible, it should be directed in the medium term towards providing a stable background and influencing the price level. But in the short run, since monetary conditions do impinge upon the course of economic activity, some flexibility in monetary policy is desirable.

Conclusion

The student who has reached this stage will have realized that there are still many unresolved questions both in the theory of monetary economics and in the conduct of monetary policy. In recent years the monetarist star has been in the ascendant, a consequence perhaps of world-wide inflationary experience. Where output cannot change quickly, the link between money and prices is most obvious when money grows fast – as has been the case for many individual countries and also on an international scale in the last decade. That a lower rate of monetary growth is a *sine qua non* for price stability is not seriously in dispute. Argument centres on how to bring this about without exposing countries to intolerable economic costs and political strains.

How far monetary policy should be employed for stabilizing economic activity in conditions of approximate price stability is still a highly contentious matter, as are the relative weights to be given to monetary aggregates as against various interest rates in guiding and implementing policy. A middle-of-the-road position would be that policy should not adhere to some fixed rule for monetary growth, but that intervention directed to smoothing economic fluctuations should be cautious and modest, in order to reduce the risk of accentuating the inherent instability of the economy. And an eclectic view would pay attention both to interest rates and monetary aggregates, giving more weight to the former in the short run when in the absence of compensating action by the authorities erratic shifts of confidence or other factors would otherwise lead to quite sharp interest rate changes, and more weight to monetary aggregates in the long run when persistent imbalances between the anticipated levels of saving and investment will be revealed.

On a theoretical plane, the distance between opposing views has in fact been narrowing, particularly in the theory of the demand for money. Differences are now more differences of emphasis than opposing views of the nature of economic processes. Since theories necessarily abstract from reality, retaining what are regarded as essential factors and rejecting inessentials, the choice of theoretical approach must depend on the circumstances in which the theory is to be deployed. In this author's view the monetarist approach can be deployed most effectively in conditions of rapid inflation and in analysis of long-run trends, when changes in output are either *comparatively* unimportant or determined independently of effective demand. The Keynesian approach and its more recent developments come into their own in the analysis of short-run cyclical behaviour, when output may fluctuate more violently than prices. Rather than accepting one theory and rejecting another, it seems more sensible to apply that theoretical approach which is best suited to the problem under scrutiny.

References

Allais, M. (1966), 'A restatement of the quantity theory of money', *Amer. econ. Rev.*, vol. 56, December, pp. 1123–57.

Andersen, L. C., and Jordan, J. L. (1968), 'Monetary and fiscal actions: a test of their relative importance in economic stabilisation', *Federal Reserve Bank of St Louis Monthly Review*, November, pp. 11–24.

Ando, A., and Modigliani, F. (1965), 'The relative stability of monetary velocity and the investment multiplier, 1897–1955', *Amer. econ. Rev.*, vol. 55, September, pp. 693–728.

Artis, M. J., and Nobay, A. R. (1969), 'Two aspects of the monetary debate', *Nat. Inst. econ. Rev.*, August, pp. 33–51.

Aschheim, J. (1963), 'Restrictive open market operations versus reserve-requirement increases: a reformulation', *Econ. J.*, vol. 73, June, pp. 254–66.

Bain, A. D. (1964), 'Monetary control through open-market operations and reserve-requirement variations', *Econ. J.*, vol. 74, March, pp. 137–46.

Bank of England (1969), 'The United Kingdom banking sector 1952–1967', *Quarterly Bulletin*, vol. 9, no. 2, pp. 176–200.

Bank of England (1969), 'Domestic credit expansion', *Quarterly Bulletin*, vol. 9, no. 3 supplement, pp. 363–82.

Bank of England (1970), *Statistical Abstract*, no. 1.

Baumol, W. (1952), 'The transactions demand for cash – an inventory theoretic approach', *Q. J. Econ.*, vol. 66, November, pp. 545–56.

Brainard, W. C., and Tobin, J. (1968), 'Pitfalls in financial model building', *Amer. econ. Rev.*, vol. 58, papers and proceedings, May, pp. 99–122

Bronfenbrenner, M., and Mayer, T. (1960), 'Liquidity functions in the American economy', *Econometrica*, vol. 28, October, pp. 810–34.

Cagan, P. (1956), 'The monetary dynamics of hyperinflation', in M. Friedman (ed.), *Studies in the Quantity Theory of Money*, Chicago University Press.

Campbell, C. D. (1970), 'The velocity of money and the rate of inflation: recent experiences in South Korea and Brazil', in D. M. Meiselman (ed.), *Varieties of Monetary Experience*, The University of Chicago Press.

Central Statistical Office, *Financial Statistics*, monthly, HMSO

Central Statistical Office (1969), 'Money supply and domestic credit', *Econ. Trends*, no. 187, May.

Commission on Money and Credit (1961), *Report*, Prentice-Hall.

Deaver, J. V. (1970), 'The Chilean inflation and the demand for money', in D. M. Meiselman (ed.), *Varieties of Monetary Experience*, The University of Chicago Press.

De Leeuw, F., and Gramlich, E. M. (1969), 'The channels of monetary policy', *Fed. Res. Bull.*, June, pp. 472–91.

Diz, A. C. (1970), 'Money and prices in Argentina, 1935–1962', in D. M. Meiselman (ed.), *Varieties of Monetary Experience*, The University of Chicago Press.

Edge, S. K. (1967), 'The relative stability of monetary velocity and the investment multiplier', *Austral. econ. Papers*, December, pp. 192–207.

Fisher, I. (1911), *The Purchasing Power of Money*, Macmillan.

Friedman, M. (1956), 'The quantity theory of money – a restatement', in *Studies in the Quantity Theory of Money*, Chicago University Press.

Friedman, M. (1957), *A Theory of the Consumption Function*, Princeton University Press.

Friedman, M. (1961), 'The lag in the effect of monetary policy', *J. Polit. Econ.*, October, pp. 447–66.

Friedman, M. (1968), 'The role of monetary policy', *Amer. econ. Rev.*, vol. 58, March, pp. 1–17.

Friedman, M., and Meiselman, D. (1963), 'The relative stability of monetary velocity and the investment multiplier', prepared for the Commission on Money and Credit, Prentice-Hall.

Friedman, M., and Schwartz, A. J. (1963a), *A Monetary History of the United States*, Princeton University Press.

Friedman, M., and Schwartz, A. J. (1963b), 'Money and business cycles', *Rev. econ. Stat.*, vol. 45, supplement, February, pp. 32–64.

Goldfeld, S. M. (1973), 'The demand for money revisited', *Brookings Papers on Economic Activity*, no. 3, pp. 577–638.

Goodhart, C. A. E. (1972), 'Analysis of the determinants of the stock of money', in M. Parkin and A. R. Nobay (eds.), *Essays in Modern Economics*, Aberystwyth.

Goodhart, C. A. E., and Crockett, A. D. (1970), 'The importance of money', *Bank of England Quarterly Bulletin*, vol. 10, no. 2, June, pp. 159–98.

Hacche, G. (1974), 'The demand for money in the United Kingdom: experience since 1971', *Bank of England Quarterly Bulletin*, vol. 14, no. 3, September, pp. 284–305.

Hilton, K., and Crossfield, D. H. (1970), 'Short-run consumption functions for the UK, 1955–66', in K. Hilton and D. F. Heathfield (eds.), *The Econometric Study of the United Kingdom*, Macmillan, pp. 59–98.

Hines, A. G., and Catephores, G. (1970), 'Investment in UK manufacturing industry, 1956–67', in K. Hilton and D. F. Heathfield (eds.), *The Econometric Study of the United Kingdom*, Macmillan, pp. 203–24.

Johnson, H. G. (1967), 'Notes on the theory of the transactions demand for cash', in *Essays in Monetary Economics*, Unwin.

Kavanagh, N. J., and Walters, A. A. (1966), 'Demand for money in the United Kingdom, 1877–1961: some preliminary findings', *Bull. Oxf. Univ. Institut. Econs. Stats.*, vol. 28, May, pp. 93–116.

Keynes, J. M. (1936), *The General Theory of Employment, Interest and Money*, Macmillan.

Laidler, D. E. W. (1966), 'The rate of interest and the demand for money – some empirical evidence', *J. Polit. Econ.*, vol. 74, December, pp. 543–55.

Laidler, D. E. W. (1969), *The Demand for Money: Theories and Evidence*, International Textbook Co.

Leijonhufvud, A. (1968), *On Keynesian Economics and the Economics of Keynes*, Oxford University Press.

McMahon, C. W. (1965), 'The techniques of economic forecasting', *OECD*.

Marshall, A. (1923), *Money, Credit and Commerce*, Macmillan.

Pigou, A. C. (1917), 'The value of money', *Q. J. Econ.*, vol. 32, November, pp. 38–65.

Radcliffe Committee on the Working of the Monetary System (1959), *Report*, Cmnd 827, HMSO.

Starleaf, D. R., and Reimer, R. (1967), 'The Keynesian demand function for money: some statistical tests', *J. Finance*, vol. 22, March, pp. 71–6.

Tobin, J. (1958), 'Liquidity preference as behaviour towards risk', *Rev. econ. Stud.*, vol. 25, February, pp. 65–86.

Tobin, J. (1969), 'A general equilibrium approach to monetary theory', *J. Money, Credit and Banking*, vol. 1, February, pp. 15–29.

Trivedi, P. K. (1970), 'Inventory behaviour in UK manufacturing, 1956–67', *Rev. econ. Stud.*, vol. 37, October, pp. 517–36.

Wallich, H. C. (1967), 'Quantity theory and quantity policy', in W. Fellner *et al.* (eds.), *Ten Economic Studies in the Tradition of Irving Fisher*, Wiley.

Walters, A. A. (1966), 'Monetary multipliers in the UK, 1880–1962', *Oxf. econ. Papers*, new series, vol. 18, November, pp. 270–83.

Index